Developing Research Skills
A Laboratory Manual
Fourth Edition

Prepared by
Helen J. Crawford
Virginia Polytechnic Institute and State University

Larry B. Christensen
University of South Alabama

Allyn and Bacon
Boston London Toronto Sydney Tokyo Singapore

ISBN 0-205-32719-2

Printed in the United States of America

10 9 8 7 6   08 09 10

CONTENTS

PREFACE

Traditional research laboratory manuals in the Behavioral Sciences emphasize the experimental approach to hypothesis testing. In *Developing Research Methods: A Laboratory Manual* we provide not only the experimental approach but also non-experimental approaches (naturalistic observation, phenomenological studies, secondary record research, survey research, correlational research, and ex post facto studies). Thus, like many research textbooks available today we emphasize a multi-method approach to hypothesis testing. This manual can easily be adapted to accompany any research methods textbook in psychology and closely allied social science areas.

The laboratory exercises within each of the topics provide students with training in how to do both experimental and non-experimental research in various settings. The exercises have been designed to train students systematically in how to use and evaluate the scientific method in psychological research. They will learn how to identify a problem and conduct a literature search, to develop hypotheses and translate them into appropriate research designs, to define variables conceptually and operationally, to choose appropriate populations for study in non-biased manners, to develop control and reduce extraneous variables, to design research, to gather and analyze data, to interpret results, and to communicate findings to others.

This manual serves both future researchers and consumers of research. It is a training ground for students who will go on to more advanced research methodology and psychology courses. Also it trains individuals to be discerning research consumers so that when they read research they will do it with a critical eye, evaluating its appropriateness and limitations.

Rather than emphasize specific content areas, we have chosen exercises that maximize student interest. Some of the exercises permit the students to learn more about themselves (a desire of many students who take psychology courses). The topics include exercises on learning styles, dreams, ESP, alcohol usage among college students, eating disorders among college students, and illusions, to name but a few.

With the explosion of the Internet since our last edition, we supplemented the various exercises with references to appropriate Internet sites and encourage students to use them. Students need to learn to be critical consumers of the Internet; thus, we provide one exercise that requires students to evaluate a psychologically-oriented Internet web site. Other exercises address directly the use of the Internet for psychological sources. These include: Topic 2: Searching the Literature; Topic 6, Laboratory Exercise 2: Internet Survey Research; and Topic 15: Analyzing Published Studies. We chose URL sites that would be fairly stable over time.

The manual is organized to provide maximum flexibility to the instructor. Alternate laboratory exercises are included in each of the fifteen topics covered in the laboratory manual. Instructors are not expected to use all of the exercises; rather, they can choose those exercises they think most appropriate for their class. For some of the topics in which actual research studies are conducted, it is suggested that different exercises be assigned to group of students within the class. For example, for Topic 6 which addresses survey research, some students could be assigned to carry out a survey on alcohol usage on campus, while others could be assigned to do a survey on the prevalence of bulimia or on attitudes towards ESP. Using our surveys, we and other instructors have had students present regional and national papers, as well as publish their work in referred journals.

The presentation order of the topics may be changed. We recommend that Topics 1 (Scientific Observation), 2 (Problem Identification and Hypothesis Testing), and 3 (Operational Definitions) come first in any course. The subsequent topics can be reorganized to fit the needs of the course. Presently the subsequent laboratory exercises are organized from the least controlled (naturalistic observations) to the most controlled (experimental) research approaches. Another logical presentation order would be to present first the topics addressing experimental research (Topics 7, 8, 9, 10, 11 and 12) and secondly those addressing descriptive research (Topics 4, 5, 6, and 7). Topic 14 addresses ethical issues and the development of consent forms and debriefing statements; this can be introduced at the appropriate time in the course. Finally, Topic 15 provides training in the evaluation of research articles, and can be presented as a single exercise or divided into separate exercises to be turned in periodically throughout the class term. Some topics may need to be eliminated due to time constraints. Certain exercises can also be used as supplementary in-class exercises for the course that accompanies the laboratory. For example, "Production of Visual Illusion Reversals" (Topic 9, Laboratory Exercise 2) is a fun, in-class demonstration of practice effects.

While many exercises direct the students as to exactly what to do and hand in to the instructor, others indicate that the instructor will tell the student what to write up. It is our experience that some instructors wish the study to be written up completely, while other instructors ask students to write up only one part of the study (for example, introduction, method, results, or discussion sections). It is left up to the instructor to decide how much of the study should be written up.

We recommend strongly that the students either purchase or have available for their use the latest edition of the Publication Manual of the American Psychological Association. In addition, it is expected that the instructor will provide guidance as to which statistics are appropriate for certain exercises. This decision depends upon the statistics background of the students. As students increasingly own their own computers or have access to them on their campuses, a number of instructors have begun to require students to use statistical packages. Online statistical tutorials can be found, such as the one at the University of California at Los Angeles (http://www.stat.ucla.edu). University of South Carolina's statistics department provides free *WebStat* data analysis software at http://www.stat.sc.edu/webstat.

We encourage instructors and students to give us feedback. If you have any suggestions for improvements, please send them to either

Helen Crawford, Department of Psychology, Virginia Polytechnic Institute and State University, Blacksburg, VA 24061; e-mail at hjc@vt.edu, or

Larry B. Christensen, Department of Psychology, University of South Alabama, Mobile, AL 36688; e-mail at lchriste@usamail.usouthal.edu.

Word of Thanks

We owe a debt of appreciation to the many people who assisted us in revising our laboratory manual. Our own students in research methods courses and the graduate teaching assistants who often oversaw the actual laboratory exercises provided excellent suggestions for improvement. Special appreciation is given to those individuals who provided formal reviews of earlier editions.

TOPIC 1: SCIENTIFIC OBSERVATION

Psychologists use the scientific method to acquire knowledge about human and animal behavior. It is a logical process or method of acquiring information that involves five major steps: identifying the problem and forming a hypothesis, designing the research, conducting the research, testing the hypotheses, and communicating the results. A researcher often does not move systematically through these steps, but rather moves back and forth (e.g., Christensen, 2001). When one uses the scientific method rather than other approaches of acquiring knowledge (tenacity, intuition, authority, rationalism and empiricism), the emphasis is upon making objective observations without bias or opinion.

Psychologists use a wide variety of techniques to carry out their scientific observations. They observe behavior either with or without the knowledge of those being observed. They may use archival material, informal observations, standardized observations, self-reports requiring open-ended responses or responses to rating scales, personality tests, cognitive and perceptual tests, neuropsychological tests, experimental tasks, physiological measures, and so on. They may carry out their research in an experimental laboratory, in a clinical setting, in the field, or they may use previously collected material as their data. These many techniques can be categorized under several research design approaches:

1. **Non-experimental Research Approach.** This approach describes accurately the phenomena being studied, but does not attempt to determine the cause-and-effect relationships between variables. Subsumed under this approach are a number of types of research: case studies, naturalistic observation, ethnographic studies, phenomenology studies, secondary record studies, field studies, surveys, correlational studies, and ex post facto studies.

2. **Experimental Research Approach.** This approach attempts to determine the cause-and-effect relationship between variables by using the psychological experiment, which is an "objective observation of phenomena which are made to occur in a strictly controlled situation in which one or more factors are varied and the others are kept constant" (Zimney, 1961, p. 18).

Two major research settings for psychological research are the laboratory and the field, although psychologists also use other settings (e.g., library for archival studies). The laboratory permits the investigator to develop more precise control over the environment, events, tasks, and stimuli to which the research participants are exposed. As the control of manipulated variables and extraneous variables increases, the researcher can be more confident about any cause-and-effect conclusions that are drawn from the results. Field research, often in a natural setting, provides the advantage of studying people as they naturally behave but often has the disadvantage of less control.

The laboratory exercises within each of the topics provided in this laboratory manual provide you with training in how to do both descriptive and experimental research in various settings. The exercises have been designed to train you systematically in how to use and evaluate the scientific method in psychological research. You will learn how to identify a problem and conduct a literature search, to develop hypotheses and translate them into appropriate research designs, to define your variables conceptually and operationally, to choose appropriate populations for study in nonbiased manners, to develop control and reduce extraneous variables, to design your procedures, to gather and analyze your data, to interpret your findings, and to communicate your findings to others. A good researcher is always improving and refining his or her research approaches. Research should be exciting and rewarding. Certainly there is always a lot of mundane and tedious daily work, as is the case in most careers, but the excitement of acquiring new knowledge and communicating it to others is worth it to the committed researcher.

While you are presently a novice, you will probably be surprised by how much you learn by the end of the course. You may not become a researcher in psychology, but you will become a much more sophisticated consumer of scientific research. When you read newspapers, magazines and Internet sites you will be able to analyze research reports critically and to evaluate the appropriateness and limitations of the research. If you are in a community organization, you will have the basic knowledge of how to design and carry out surveys and to communicate their results to others.

With the guidance of our own students in past research methods classes we, the authors of this laboratory manual, have chosen and refined what we think to be interesting and relevant exercises. So often we have had psychology students complain that they do not learn enough about themselves in the process of studying psychology (and, yet, that is one of the major reasons many students take psychology courses!). For that reason, we have included several exercises that are aimed at learning more about yourself. The first laboratory exercise below is just such an exercise.

Psychology has conducted thousands of experiments on learning and retention of material and developed major theories about learning and memory. While many of us think we are efficiently reading and retaining information, we may not be as efficient as we could be. The first exercise is aimed at helping you understand your own learning style, its strengths and weaknesses, while at the same time demonstrating that science requires objective observations. A comparison of learning strategies with grade point average will be made. While the exercise is correlational in nature, we hope it will encourage you to think of how you might change your learning strategies to improve your ability to gain knowledge (and improve your grades!).

Laboratory Exercises 2 and 3 provide additional examples illustrating the necessity of objective observation by involving you as an active participant in the recall of your own dreams.

References:

Christensen, L. B. (2001). *Experimental psychology* (8th ed.). Boston: Allyn and Bacon, Inc.
Zimney, G. H. (1961). *Method in experimental psychology*. New York: Ronald Press.

LABORATORY EXERCISE 1: RELATIONSHIP BETWEEN LEARNING STYLES AND GRADE POINT AVERAGE

The purpose of this laboratory exercise is to determine the relationship between various learning styles and cumulated grade point average.

Before proceeding with the reading of this laboratory exercise, turn to the end of this exercise. Fill out the Inventory of Learning Processes (Schmeck, 1983) as honestly as you can. When you have completed the inventory, turn to the following page in this exercise where directions are given as to how it is to be scored. Score your inventory and anonymously turn your scores in to your instructor.

We do not all study or comprehend information in the same manner. Different students use different strategies when reading or listening to information. Some individuals tend to think deeply and elaboratively while others think shallowly and reiteratively while reading, studying, or listening to a lecture. Human learning and memory research suggests that individuals who process information deeply and elaboratively recall more information than those who do not. Craik and Lockhart (1972) first proposed that there were levels of processing, falling on a continuum from shallow (information is repeated) to deep (meanings and associations are evaluated).

Individuals do better on laboratory tasks if they process information deeply and elaboratively. Research indicates that such a relationship is found in applied settings, such as classrooms. Several inventories were developed which assess various learning styles. The one we are interested in, the Inventory of Learning Processes, was developed by Ronald Schmeck and his colleagues at Southern Illinois University. This inventory is made up of 62 true-false statements concerned with learning activities within the school environment. Different learning styles are reflected in four scales:

(1) <u>Deep Processing</u>. Consisting of 18 items, this scale assesses "the extent to which students critically evaluate, conceptually organize, and compare and contrast the information they study" (Schmeck, 1983, p. 245).

(2) <u>Elaborative Processing</u>. Consisting of 14 items, this scale assesses "the extent to which students translate new information into their own terminology, generate concrete examples from their own experience, apply new information to their own lives, and use visual imagery to encode new ideas" (Schmeck, 1983, p. 248).

(3) <u>Fact Retention</u>. Consisting of 7 items, this scale assesses how carefully individuals "process (and thus store) details and specific pieces of new information regardless of what other information-processing strategies they might employ" (Schmeck, 1983, p. 248).

(4) <u>Methodical Study</u>. Consisting of 23 items, this scale assesses the degree to which individuals "claim to study more often and more carefully than other students, and the methods that they claim to employ (that) are the systematic techniques recommended in all of the old 'how to study' manuals (e.g., 'type your notes, outline the text, study everyday in the same location, make up practice tests, etc.')" (Schmeck, 1983, p. 249).

The intercorrelations between the four scales indicate that Deep Processing and Elaborative Processing are the most closely related. Craik and Tulving (1975) argue that these are the most important ways to improve memory. They do differ somewhat in that they predict different, although related, performances. Schmeck (1983) reported that various studies show that Deep Processing is related to critical thinking ability, reading comprehension, verbal ability, attention to the semantic attributes of words, and the Wechsler Adult Intelligence Test's digit-span subtest. The Elaborative Processing scale is related to writing performance, use of mental imagery, subjective organization of recalled word lists, and the tendency to organize work lists around rhymes. Schmeck (1983) reported that "the person who scores high on Fact Retention is prone to follow instructions carefully, to be bound by the course syllabus, and to process details, while the person who scores high on Elaborative Processing is able to elaborate and personalize information verbally as well as through imagery" (p. 252). Schmeck and his colleagues have found that the person who scores high on Methodical Study is achievement striving "of the <u>conforming</u> sort (which) suggests that these students are eager to please and are bound by the course syllabus" (pp. 251-252). In a clinical study, deep elaborative students were rated as "clearer, deeper, and more conclusion-oriented and personal" when discussing personal problems with counselors (McCarthy, Shaw, & Schmeck, 1986).

College students who have high grade point averages (GPAs) score significantly higher on the Deep Processing subscale than those with average or low GPAs (Bartling, 1988; Gadzella, Ginther, & Williamson, 1986; Miller, Alway, & McKinley, 1987: Schmeck & Grove, 1979). Students with high GPAs and high American College Test (ACT) assessment scores tend to score high on deep processing, elaborative processing, and fact retention (Schmeck & Grove, 1979). While GPA was not correlated with Methodical Study, low ACT scorers scored significantly higher on Methodical Study than did high ACT scorers. Such relationships between these learning styles and academic performance is not attributable to intelligence differences (Schmeck, 1983).

For your laboratory exercise, compute the correlation between the four learning style scales and cumulated grade point average for the students in your class. Below are some means for each of the scales, taken from Schmeck (1983). Compare your own scores and the class' means with them.

	Deep Processing	Elaborative Processing	Fact Retention	Methodical Study
Low GPA students	10.40	9.80	4.26	10.15
High GPA students	12.58	10.53	5.11	10.57

Your instructor may require you to read some of the references provided below. Schmeck, Geisler-Brenstein, and Cercy (1991) have revised the Inventory of Learning Process. You may wish to explore how it has been revised and expanded.

As a class discussion, you may wish to discuss methods that might improve your learning habits and, hopefully, your academic performance.

Your instructor will direct you as to how to write up this exercise.

Learning Style References:

Bartling, C. A. (1988). Longitudinal changes in the study habits of successful college students. *Educational and Psychological Measurement, 48,* 527-535.

Beyler, J., & Schmeck, R. R. (1992). Assessment of individual differences in preferences for holistic-analytics strategies: Evaluation of some commonly available instruments. *Educational and Psychological Measurement, 52,* 709-719.

Craik, F. I. M., & Lockhart, R. S. (1972). Levels of processing: A framework for memory research. *Journal of Verbal Learning and Verbal Behavior, 11,* 671-684.

Gadzelle, B. M., Ginther, D. W., Williamson, J. D. (1986). Differences in learning processes and academic achievement. *Perpetual and Motor Skills, 62,* 151-156.

Hermann, D. J. (1982). Know they memory: The use of questionnaires to assess and study memory. *Psychological Bulletin, 92,* 434-452.

McCarthy, P. R., Shaw, T., & Schmeck, R. R. (1986). Behavioral analysis of client learning during counseling. *Journal of Counseling Psychology, 33,* 249-254.

Miller, C. D., Alway, M., & McKinley, D. L. (1987). Effects of learning styles and strategies on academic success. *Journal of College Student Personnel, 28,* 399-404.

Schmeck, R. R. (1983). Learning styles of college students. In R. Dillon, & R. Schmeck (Eds.), *Individual differences in cognition.* New York: Academic Press.

Schmeck, R. R., & Geisler-Brenstein, E. (1989). Individual differences that affect the way students approach learning. *Learning and Individual Differences, 1,* 85-124.

Schmeck, R. R., Geisler-Brenstein, E., & Cercy, S. P. (1991). Self-concept and learning: The revised Inventory of Learning Processes. *Educational Psychology, 11,* 343-362.

Schmeck, R. R., & Grove, E. (1979). Academic achievement and individual differences in learning processes. *Applied Psychological Measurement, 3,* 43-49.

Schmeck, R. R., & Meier, S. T. (1984). Self-reference as a learning strategy and a learning style. *Human Learning, 3,* 9-17.

Schmeck, R. R., & Phillips, J. (1982). Levels of processing as dimension of difference between individuals. *Human Learning, 1,* 95-103.

Schmeck, R. R., Ribich, F. D., & Ramanaiah, N. (1977). Development of a self-report inventory for assessing individual differences in learning processes. *Applied Psychological Measurement, 1,* 413-431.

Inventory of Learning Processes

This questionnaire asks you to describe the way you study and learn. There are many different ways to study and learn, any of which may be effective for a particular individual. Since this is the case, there are no "right" or "wrong" answers to these questions. We are simply trying to find out the ways in which people learn best. If we are successful in this we may be able to help instructors design their courses with student needs and competencies in mind. This instrument could also help counselors advise students as to what courses to take and how to study for them.

Answer TRUE or FALSE to each statement in the questionnaire. If a particular statement applies to you, check TRUE. If a particular statement does not apply to you, check FALSE. In answering each question, try to think in terms of how you go about learning in general, rather than thinking of a specific course or subject area. Be accurate and honest in your answers. Be sure to complete all the items, but do not spend a great deal of time on any one of them This survey is for research use only and all information is kept confidential.

	TRUE	FALSE
1. When studying for an exam, I prepare a list of probable questions and answers.	___	___
2. I have trouble making inferences.	___	___
3. I increase my vocabulary by building lists of new terms.	___	___
4. I am very good at learning formulas, names and dates.	___	___
5. New concepts usually make me think of many other similar concepts.	___	___
6. Even when I feel that I have learned the material, I continue to study.	___	___
7. I have trouble organizing the information that I remember.	___	___
8. Even when I know I have carefully learned the material, I have trouble remembering it for an exam.	___	___
9. After reading a unit of material, I sit and think about it.	___	___
10. I make simple charts and diagrams to help me remember material.	___	___
11. I generally write an outline of the material I read.	___	___
12. I try to convert facts into "rules of thumb".	___	___
13. I do well on tests requiring definitions.	___	___
14. I usually refer to several sources in order to understand a concept.	___	___
15. I ignore conflicts between the information obtained from different sources.	___	___
16. I spend more time studying than most of my friends.	___	___

17. I learn new words or ideas by visualizing a situation in which they occur. ____ ____

18. I learn new concepts by expressing them in my own words. ____ ____

19. I often memorize material that I do not understand. ____ ____

20. For examinations, I memorize the material as given in the text or class notes. ____ ____

21. I carefully complete all course assignments. ____ ____

22. I have difficulty planning work when confronted with a complex task. ____ ____

23. I remember new words and ideas by associating them with words and ideas
   I already know. ____ ____

24. I review course material periodically during the quarter. ____ ____

25. I often have difficulty finding the right words for expressing my ideas. ____ ____

26. Toward the end of a course, I prepare an overview of all material covered. ____ ____

27. I find it difficult to handle questions requiring comparison of different concepts. ____ ____

28. I generally read beyond what is assigned in class. ____ ____

29. I have difficulty learning how to study for a course. ____ ____

30. I have a regular place to study. ____ ____

31. I read critically. ____ ____

32. I "daydream" about things I have studied. ____ ____

33. I do well on completion items. ____ ____

34. I make frequent use of a dictionary. ____ ____

35. I learn new ideas by relating them to similar ideas. ____ ____

36. When learning a unit of material, I usually summarize it in my own words. ____ ____

37. I maintain a daily schedule of study hours. ____ ____

38. I think. ____ ____

39. While learning new concepts their practical applications often come to my mind. ____ ____

40. I get good grades on term papers. ____ ____

41. Getting myself to begin studying is usually difficult. ____ ____

42. When necessary, I can easily locate particular passages in a textbook. ____ ____

43. I can usually formulate a good guess even when I do not know the answer. ____ ____

44. I have trouble remembering definitions. ____ ____

45. I would rather read the original article than a summary of an article. ____ ____

46. While studying, I attempt to find answers to questions I have in mind. ____ ____

46. I can usually state the underlying message of films and readings. ____ ____

48. I work through practice exercises and sample problems. ____ ____

49. I find it difficult to handle questions requiring critical evaluation. ____ ____

50. I have regular weekly review periods. ____ ____

51. I do well on examinations requiring much factual information. ____ ____

52. Most of my instructors lecture too fast. ____ ____

53. I look for reasons behind the facts. ____ ____

54. I cram for exams. ____ ____

55. When I study something, I devise a system for recalling it later. ____ ____

56. I have trouble seeing the difference between apparently similar ideas. ____ ____

57. I always make a special effort to get all the details. ____ ____

58. I prepare a set of notes integrating the information from all sources in a course. ____ ____

59. My memory is actually pretty poor. ____ ____

60. I am usually able to design procedures for solving problems. ____ ____

61. I do well on essay tests. ____ ____

62. I frequently use the library. ____ ____

*Inventory of Learning Processes (Schmeck, 1983), by permission of the author.

Scoring Sheet for Inventory of Learning Processes

Give yourself one point for each statement that is TRUE or FALSE as indicated. For instance, if you answered FALSE to item #2, give yourself 1 point. If you answered TRUE, give yourself 0. When you have completed each of the four scales, add them up for a total score.

After you have scored each scale, double check your scoring. Finally, add each column for a total score for each scale.

SCALE 1:		SCALE 2:		SCALE 3:		SCALE 4:	
DEEP PROCESSING		**ELABORATIVE PROCESSING**		**FACT RETENTION**		**METHODICAL STUDY**	
2. FALSE	____	5. TRUE	____	4. TRUE	____	1. TRUE	____
7. FALSE	____	9. TRUE	____	13. TRUE	____	3. TRUE	____
8. FALSE	____	12. TRUE	____	20. TRUE	____	6. TRUE	____
15. FALSE	____	17. TRUE	____	33. TRUE	____	10. TRUE	____
19. FALSE	____	18. TRUE	____	44. FALSE	____	11. TRUE	____
22. FALSE	____	23. TRUE	____	51. TRUE	____	14. TRUE	____
25. FALSE	____	32. TRUE	____	59. FALSE	____	16. TRUE	____
27. FALSE	____	35. TRUE	____			21. TRUE	____
29. FALSE	____	36. TRUE	____			24. TRUE	____
31. TRUE	____	39. TRUE	____			26. TRUE	____
38. TRUE	____	46. TRUE	____			28. TRUE	____
40. TRUE	____	53. TRUE	____			30. TRUE	____
43. TRUE	____	55. TRUE	____			34. TRUE	____
47. TRUE	____	60. TRUE	____			37. TRUE	____
49. FALSE	____					41. FALSE	____
52. FALSE	____					42. TRUE	____
56. FALSE	____					45. TRUE	____
61. TRUE	____					48. TRUE	____
	____					50. TRUE	____
						54. FALSE	____
						57. TRUE	____
						58. TRUE	____
						62. TRUE	____

_____		_____		_____		_____	
TOTAL SCALE 1		**TOTAL SCALE 2**		**TOTAL SCALE 3**		**TOTAL SCALE 4**	

OVERALL GRADE POINT AVERAGE: _____

GENDER: MALE ____   FEMALE ____

AGE: _____

Turn this form into your instructor when it is completed. Do not put your name on it.

LABORATORY EXERCISE 2: RECALL OF DREAMS

The purpose of Laboratory Exercise 2 is to demonstrate how dream researchers collect dream reports from participants at home and how dream recall can be assisted by following a few simple suggestions. In Laboratory Exercise 3 you will do a content analysis of your dreams.

For the night your instructor assigns, you are to write down in detail all the dreams you recall during that night. Bring your description of your dreams to the assigned class period for discussion.

To assist yourself in dream recall, do the following:

1. Tell yourself before you go to sleep: "I shall remember all of my dreams tonight. It will be easy to write them down during the night or in the morning when I wake up."

2. Have paper and pencil next to your bed so that you can easily record your dreams.

3. When you wake up, do not move. Keep your eyes closed and review your dreams while you remain in your drowsy state. After you have reviewed your dreams, write them down.

4. If you cannot remember your dreams, set your alarm clock to go off 90 minutes after you go to sleep. This should wake you up during your first dream cycle.

For each of the dreams you recall, do the following:

1. Write each dream in as much detail as possible, in present or past tense.

2. If there are parts of the dream that you do not remember, just indicate that there are parts not remembered.

3. Describe the emotions and feelings that were in the dream, both your own and others.

4. After you have completed the description, read the dream over slowly and determine if you can remember anything else. If so, record it.

5. On a separate sheet of paper, write down how you react to this dream. Does it remind you of something? Was something from the previous day incorporated into it?

6. Finally, write down what you think is (are) the meaning(s) of the dream. Is it related to anything you did or said in the past few days? Is it related to any events in the past? Is it about any upcoming events in the future?

7. When you have finished 1-6 for each of your dreams, on a separate page, describe any connections you think may exist between your dreams.

Participant observation can be biased. Think about how you may have only partially recalled the dreams or actively censured your written report.

LABORATORY EXERCISE 3: CONTENT ANALYSIS OF DREAMS

The purpose of Laboratory Exercise 3 is to give you some experience in analyzing the content of dreams.

The exciting realm of sleep and dreams is something we all experience, yet often know little about. In this lab we will address "What is in a dream?" This simple question has stimulated many observations, studies, and theories. When we tell our dreams to others, it not unusual to censure it as a large number of social factors influence the reporting of dreams (Cartwright & Kasniak, 1978). This is a potential confound in dream research. The content may be influenced by societal expectations too. For instance, the Cuna Indians on the San Blas Islands off Panama collectively shared their dreams and their content influenced subsequent work activities (Van de Castle, 1994).

The first systematic studies of dream content were of blind participants in 1838 and 1888 (Van de Castle, 1994). Mary Calkins, a psychologist at Wellesley College and the first female president of the American Psychological Association, published the first systematic investigation of sensory imagery in dreams of healthy individuals in 1893. She observed a connection between waking and dream life in 89 percent of hundreds of dreams collected from herself and another person. Up until today, dream researchers study the content of home and sleep laboratory dream reports from college students (e.g., Hall & Van de Castle, 1966b; Hall, Domhoff, Blick, & Weesner, 1982), children (Foulkes, 1999) and other groups.

Hall et al. (1982) posed the question whether college students of the 1980s dreamt about the same things as their counterparts 30 years earlier when Hall and Van de Castle (1966b) asked students to keep dream diaries. They used some of the Hall-Van de Castle (1966a) scales of dream content: "characters; aggressive, friendly, and sexual interactions; misfortunes; settings; and two types of objects, clothing and weapons" (p. 189). They found that dreams of middle- and upper-middle class college students in 1950 and 1980 were quite similar in content. Somewhat surprisingly, the gender differences in the 1980 sample were the same as those in the 1950 sample. In Table 1 some of the proportions for their dream categories are presented. A proportion was determined by dividing the top number of the formula by the bottom one. For instance, to determine the proportion of male characters in a dream one would take the total number of male characters and divide that by the total number of both male and female characters (Males/Males + Females). If there were an equal number of men and women it would be .50; if there were more men than women, it would be greater than .50. Now look at Table 1. You will find that men in both samples have proportions of .67; this means that the male participants reported more male than female characters. By contrast, the female participants reported significantly fewer male characters. In the Table the subscripts a and b show at what probability level (.001 or .01) the studies found significant gender differences. You should now be able to interpret the other categories of dream content.

For one or more of your dreams (as assigned by the instructor), you are to do a content analysis. This means that you are to read through your description and determine for each dream: (1) the number of male and female characters that were present in your dream; (2) the presence and number of verbal and physical aggressions there were; (3) the number of male and female characters who were doing the aggression; (4) whether there was some sort of sexual activity present; (5) whether misfortunes were present; (6) whether the settings were inside or outside; and (7) whether weapons were present. Use the worksheet provided at the end of this laboratory exercise to record your tallies.

When this is completed, develop proportions for each of the categories, following the formulas which are presented at the bottom of the worksheet. Are your dream contents similar to the norms in Table 1?

As a class project, you may wish to determine the average proportions of all your classmates and compare these averages with those presented in Table 1. An experimental question is whether similar gender differences will occur some 20 years later. You may wish to examine more recent studies (e.g., Bursik, 1998; Domhoff, 1999; Lortie-Lussier, Simond, Rinfred, & de Koninck, 1992; Schredl, Sahin, & Schaefer, 1998). Schneider and Domoff's Internet site on dreams is http://dreamresearch.net.

Three excellent Internet sites on dreams, sleep and sleep disorders are the following:

What is sleep and why do we need it?   http://faculty.washington.edu/chudler/sleep.html
NIH's National Center on Sleep Disorders Research http://rover.nhlbi.nih.gov/about/ncsdr/
A link to all sleep information on the Internet   http://www.sleepnet.com/index.shtml

Sleep References:
Antrobus, J. (1991). Dreaming: Cognitive processes during cortical activation and high afferent thresholds. *Psychological Review*, *98*, 96-121.
Bursik, K. (1998). Moving beyond gender differences: Gender role comparisons of manifest dream content. *Sex Roles, 38*, 203-214.
Calkins, M. (1893). Statistics of dreams. *American Journal of Psychology, 5*, 311-343.
Cartwright, R. L., & Kasniak, A. (1978). The social psychology of dream reporting. In A. M. Arkin, J. S. Antrobus, & S. J. Ellman (Eds.), *The mind in sleep*. Hillsdale, NJ: Lawrence Erlbaum.
Cipolli, C., Baroncini, P., Fagioli, I., Fumai, A., et al. (1987). The thematic continuity of mental sleep experience in the same night. *Sleep, 10*, 473-479.
Domhoff, G. W. (1999). New directions in the study of dream content using the Hall and Van de Castle coding system. *Dreaming: Journal of the Association for the Study of Dreams, 9*, 115-137.
Fitch, T., & Armitage, R. (1989). Variations in cognitive style among high and low frequency dream recallers. *Personality and Individual Differences, 10*, 869-875.
Foulkes, W. D. (1985). *Dreaming: A cognitive-psychological analysis*. Hillsdale, NJ: Lawrence Erlbaum Associates.
Foulkes, D. (1999). *Children's dreaming and the development of consciousness.* Cambridge, MA: Harvard University Press.
Freud, S. (1953). *The interpretation of dreams*. New York: Basic Books.
Hall, C. S. (1984). "A ubiquitous sex difference in dreams" revisited. *Journal of Personality and Social Psychology, 46*, 1109-1117.
Hall, C. S., Domhoff, W., Blick, K. A., & Weesner, K. E. (1982). The dreams of college men and women in 1950 and 1980: A comparison of dream contents and sex differences. *Sleep, 5*, 188-194.
Hall, C. S., & Van de Castle, R. L. (1966a). *The content analysis of dreams*. New York: Appleton-Century-Crofts.
Hall, C. S., & Van de Castle, R. L. (1966b). Studies of dreams collected in the laboratory and at home. *Institute of Dream Research Monograph Series*, No. 1. Felton, CA: Big Tree Press.
Hobson, J. A. (1988). *The dreaming brain*. New York: Basic Books.
Lortie-Lussier, M.,. Simond, S., Rinfred, N., & de Koninck, J. (1992). Beyond sex differences: Family and occupational roles' impact on women's and men's dreams. *Sex Roles, 26*, 79-96
Schredl, M., Sahin, V., Schaefer, G. (1998). Gender differences in dreams: Do they reflect gender differences in waking life? *Personality and Individual Differences, 25*, 433-442.
Van de Castle, R. L. (1994). *Our dreaming mind*. New York: Ballantine Boo.s
Wood, J. M., Bootzin, R. R., Rosenhan, D., Nolen-Hoeksema, S., & Jourden, F. (1992). Effects of the 1989 San Francisco earthquake on frequency and content of nightmares. *Journal of Abnormal Psychology, 101*, 219-224.

TABLE 1

Comparisons of 1950 Men and Women with 1980 Men and Women*

Content Variable	1950 STUDENTS		1980 STUDENTS	
	Men	Women	Men	Women
Characters				
1. Males/Males + Females	0.67	0.48[a]	0.67	0.53[a]
2. Familiar/Familiar + Unfamiliar	0.45	0.58[a]	0.55	0.62[a]
Aggression				
1. Aggression/Characters	0.34	0.24[a]	0.32	0.23[b]
2. Aggression with males/Males	0.28	0.22[a]	0.30	0.23[b]
3. Aggression with females/Females	0.17	0.14	0.13	0.15
4. Physical aggression/Physical + verbal aggression	0.50	0.34[a]	0.57	0.39[a]
Friendliness				
1. Friendliness/Characters	0.21	0.22	0.16	0.17
2. Friendliness with Males/Males	0.17	0.24[a]	0.09	0.20[a]
3. Friendliness with Females/ Females	0.29	0.15[a]	0.28	0.15[a]
Sex, misfortunes, settings, & objects				
1. Dreamers with at least one sex/ No. dreamers	0.38	0.17[a]	0.24	0.10[b]
2. Misfortunes/No. dreams	0.41	0.41	0.36	0.43
3. Outdoor settings/Outdoor + Indoor	0.51	0.39[a]	0.49	0.37[a]
4. Clothes/No. dreams	0.28	0.54[a]	0.10	0.34[a]
5. Weapons/No. dreams	0.12	0.03[a]	0.15	0.04[a]

a $p < 0.001$, b $p < 0.01$

*Adapted from Hall et al. (1982, p. 192, Table 2) with permission of Raven Press.

Content Analysis of Your Dreams

Category	Dream 1	Dream 2	Dream 3	Proportion*
Characters:				
Number of Males				
Number of Females				
Total				
Aggression: Type				
Number of verbal aggressions				
Number of physical aggressions				
Total				
Aggression: number of				
Males involved				
Females involved				
Total				
Sexual activity of some sort present				
Misfortunes present				
Settings:				
Indoor				
Outdoor				
Total				
Weapons Present				

* To determine proportions:

1) # of males/males + females
2) # of females/males + females
3) Aggressions/# of dreams
4) Sexual activity/# of dreams

5) Misfortunes/# of dreams
6) Indoor/indoor + outdoor
7) Outdoor/indoor + outdoor
8) # of dreams with weapons/# of dreams

GENDER: MALE ____   FEMALE _____

Turn this form into your instructor when it is completed. Do not put your name on it.

TOPIC 2: PROBLEM IDENTIFICATION AND HYPOTHESIS TESTING

The goals of Topic 2 are to provide you with instruction in conducting a literature review and to give you practice in conducting a limited literature review. Additionally, you will learn how to formulate a research question and hypothesis based upon this review. You will be encouraged to use the Internet in your searches. Finally, because there are so many Internet web sites that provide psychological information that you might use in doing background research, you are provided with an exercise to help you learn how to better evaluate an Internet web site.

You should take advantage of your librarians and any resources they have developed for your use. For instance, at Virginia Tech our students (and you) can access help on how to do library research at http://www.lib.vt.edu/research/libinst/library_research.html. Most colleges have similar sites.

When preparing to do research, scientists should conduct a thorough review of the pertinent literature contained in journal articles, books, and dissertations. While the sources of our ideas for psychological experiments come from many places, we need to know what is and is not known about the research area. The literature review helps to sharpen the experimental question so that it can be transformed into a testable experimental hypothesis.

The body of the psychological literature is enormous, containing a tremendous number of journals and books. Fortunately there are indexes available which have summarized and categorized much of this literature. When conducting a literature review, psychologists often find the most valuable index sources to be *Psychological Abstracts, Index Medicus, Social Sciences Citation Index,* and *Science Citation Index*. Computerized literature searches using each of these indexes are now available. An introduction to each of these indexes is provided below.

The major advantage of computerized literature searches is speed. A keyword search accesses the computer's memory, scanning and pulling up all titles and abstracts of articles that have the keyword(s) within them. For the most efficient and indepth search, you will probably use two or more keywords. The accompanying thesaurus is of major assistance to your determining appropriate keywords. That computerized searches are limited to the choice of keywords put in can be considered a potential disadvantage.

PSYCHOLOGICAL ABSTRACTS AND PsycINFO

Psychological Abstracts is issued monthly in journal form by the American Psychological Association. It contains brief abstracts of studies, as well as references to books, book chapters, technical reports and dissertations. The *Abstracts* has been the primary source of information about psychological literature since 1927. An earlier publication, the *Psychological Index,* covers literature published between 1894 and 1935. *PsycINFO* is an abstract database of psychological literature from 1887 to the present that is available on CD-ROM or through Internet access via your library. More information about PsycINFO can be obtained at the following site: http:www.apa.org/psychoinfo/.

In order to know where to look in the *Psychological Abstracts* or PsycINFO, since the literature is categorized under many headings, it is important to use the *Thesaurus of Psychological Index Terms*, which is also published by the American Psychological Association. The *Thesaurus* will help you identify terms and headings related to your research topic. "Each *Thesaurus* is listed alphabetically and, as appropriate, is cross-referenced and displayed with its broader, narrower, and related terms (i.e., subterms)" (APA, 1994, p. vii). The posting note (PN) indicates how many times the term has been used. The scope notes (SN) define the term. In addition, broader (B), narrower (N), and related (R) terms are provided.

If you were interested in dreaming, two general topic areas that probably came to your mind immediately are dreams and sleep. In the eighth edition of the *Thesaurus of Psychological Index Terms* (APA, 1997), the relationship section provides many headings that are related to dreaming and sleep. Look them up. The following major categories (with additional subcategories) are dream analysis, dream content, dream interpretation, dream recall, dreaming, sleep, sleep apnea, sleep deprivation, sleep disorders, sleep onset, sleep talking, sleep treatment, sleep wake cycle, and sleepwalking.

Once you have determined which subject headings will be helpful to you in your literature review, you can turn to *Psychological Abstracts* or *PsycINFO*.

In the hardback version of *Psychological Abstracts*, at the end of the monthly edition you will find both an author and subject index, with numbers following headings. The headings are those found in the *Thesaurus of Psychological Index Terms*. These numbers refer to the abstract (not page) number in that issue. You would then look up each of the numbers to read the abstract associated with it. If you wish to search literature that is older, there is an easier way than searching each month separately. You would use the Annual Index of *Psychological Abstracts*.

In the computerized version of PsychINFO, you would list those subject headings or other terms in the search engine. There are various PsychINFO database vendors and they are listed on the APA site: http://www.apa.org/psycinfo/products/vendors-all.html. Each of them vary a little from one another; thus, it is important that you find guidelines for the one your library uses. In Tables 1 and 2 are general instructions in how to use *PsycINFO*. Once the computer chooses the pertinent articles you are informed how many were found. You can then view each reference, with or without the accompanying abstract. Often you can either download the references to your own diskette for subsequent personal use or print out the information to any online printer. Please remember that all information retrieval systems are copyrighted by the individual publisher and any redistribution of the data other than for personal use must be by permission of the publisher.

The abstract provides much information. It tells you who authored the paper and where they are located (or where they were located when the research was carried out), the title of the paper, and where and when it was published. The abstract gives you a good summary of the article. There is a general statement of its purpose, how it was carried out, what the major results were, and often a theoretical interpretation of the major findings. In Table 3 is an example of how a journal abstract looks in PsychINFO for the OVID vender.

One question frequently asked by students is "How far back must I search?" The answer depends upon how extensive of a search you need to do. Ideally, you should go back as far as there is relevant material.

CUMULATED INDEX MEDICUS and MEDLINE

The National Library of Medicine publishes a *Cumulated Index Medicus* and monthly *Index Medicus* in much the same manner as *Psychological Abstracts*. It is a comprehensive index of the world's medical literature which has author and subject indexes. The National Library of Medicine offers free Internet access to MEDLINE through the use of two complimentary search engines: PubMed and Internet Grateful Med. The Internet site is http://www.nlm.nih.gov/databases/freemedl.html. This is an excellent alternative site for many areas of psychology, including personality, clinical psychology, neuropsychology, biological psychology, and the neurosciences. An advanced command searching guide for MEDLINE can be found at http://bagel.aecom.yu.edu/medline/mdlnadv.htm. Since psychology often overlaps with the medical and biological fields, MEDLINE is crucial to know as well.

SCIENCE CITATION INDEX AND SOCIAL SCIENCE CITATION INDEX

The Institute for Scientific Information's *Web of Science* (http://www.webofscience.com/) has several databases that provide over fifty years of bibliographic and citation data. The *Science Citation Index Expanded* is an interdisciplinary work covering articles in science, medicine, agriculture, technology and the behavioral sciences. Its companion series, the *Social Sciences Citation Index*, covers psychological literature as well as other social science areas. A third one is the *Arts & Humanities Citation Index*. These sources are available as hard bound books, CD-ROM, or via subscribed Internet access. Check with your library as to which they offer. Further information can be obtained from your librarian. You can do a topic search, a person search or a place search. The three section are:

A.   Permuterm Subject Index. This index should be used first in any literature search as it gives the significant terms for the titles of every article covered in the given index period. In other words, it pairs every two significant terms from each title written. If you are interested in state-dependent learning, you would look up "learning" and scan the words listed under it for "state-dependent". The names of authors who have published articles with these two terms in their titles will be listed. If your library has the Citation Indexes on CD-ROM or via the Internet, your research is made more effortless. All you need to do is write in the significant terms, "learning" and "state-dependent" in this instance, and the computer will print out a bibliography.

B.   Source Index. This index gives you full bibliographic information by author, for all articles and books written and indexed during the year currently covered. You are given the author's mailing address, the complete reference, and its complete referencing, as well as the number of references there are in each article.

C.   Citation Index. This Index lists all authors whose previous words were cited during the year covered. Every article that has made reference to an author's earlier article will be listed.

A separate, but related work is the *Index to Scientific Reviews*. This is an excellent place to start a review of the literature as it indexes solely the comprehensive review articles.

The Twelve Steps of Electronic Searching

1. State your research topic as a single question (e.g., "Does physical fitness improve sleep?").

2. Identify the separate concepts that make up the question.

3. Use the electronic Thesaurus or the Mapping feature to find descriptors that represent the first concept. Be sure to include narrower terms.

4. If you do not find relevant descriptors, search free-text words and phrases instead.

5. Use OR to combine all descriptors or free-text terms that represent the concept.

6. Repeat steps 3 through 5 for each remaining concept in your search question.

7. Use AND to combine the sets that represent the main concepts.

8. Review some of the retrieved records to assess their relevance.

9. If necessary, revise your search strategy and repeat the search.

10. Limit by language, publication year, publication type, document type, etc., as desired.

11. Select the most relevant records in your search.

12. Print or download your selected records.

About Databases and Search Systems

A database search requires a partnership between the database publisher and the system that delivers the database to you. The database publisher (PsycINFO) provides the content, selecting primary documents to include in the database and adding information that will enable you to find the article or book and to decide if the primary document is relevant to your research.

Many different service providers offer access to PsycINFO. Although the database looks quite different from one system to another, the basic information provided in each record is the same. The delivery system provides the search interface and the functions that you can employ to find the records you want.

Some search systems provide sophisticated features, such as term mapping, that make it easier to do your search. Click here to learn which of these features are available on your system. PsycINFO has also produced vendor-specific search guides with detailed information about each of the search systems on which the databases are found.

Note: The search examples in this section use generic symbols. * means truncation – all words beginning with that stem are searched (parent*). *In <field name>* means the word or phrase should be qualified to that field.

How a Bibliographic Database Search Fits Into a Research Plan

A search of a bibliographic database is the first step in investigating a new research area or refining a research project. Surveying the previous research enables you to pinpoint topics for further research or replication of that research. You can also use a search to locate general articles and books on your topic to broaden your understanding of it and to learn about recent developments.

After your research is complete, you can use a bibliographic search as an efficient way to find articles on your topic that were published since your initial search, in order to incorporate these recent findings into your report.

What You Need to Know About a Database

What kinds of documents are included?

Journals, books, etc.

Print, electronic

Scholarly or popular

What are the criteria for selecting documents?

What publication years are covered?

How often is the database updated?

Geographic coverage of documents

Languages

What information is provided in each record?

What You Need to Know About your Search System

How to navigate: select/change databases, search, display, print or download records

Where to find system help. Where to find database help

How to search specific PsycINFO fields, such as authors, titles, journals

Does the system group some subject fields for more efficient searching?

Does the system have positional operators that allow you to search one word within a given number of words from another?

What is the list of "stop words," common words that are not searched? How does this affect searches on subjects like "Type A personality?"

How do you truncate (search word stems to get variations)? Are different symbols used for one-character vs. unlimited truncation?

What special search features does the system offer, such as electronic Thesaurus, mapping of concepts to Thesaurus terms, linking to local full-text holdings or to electronic full-text, natural-language searching, linking between a book and its chapters, or ability to use PsycINFO Expert Searches?

How do you display search output in print or electronically?

How do you monitor the database to find current records on your topic?

<u>Steps in a Subject Search</u>

1. **State the search question and identify the concepts**

2. **Develop a list of search terms and fields in which to search**

3. **Locate *Thesaurus* terms for each concept**

4. **Search concepts with no *Thesaurus* terms free-text**

5. **Searching for names as subjects**

6. **Add terms from the population fields**

7. **Combine the terms for each concept**

8. **Combine the concepts**

<u>State the search question and identify the concepts</u>
Write out the search question in the most specific terms you can think of. Sometimes it helps to envision a title for the most relevant article you could find. Generally the form of the question will be "The effect of a on b in c population," Then identify the main concepts in the search question. Ignore words that describe relationships among concepts, such as effect and correlation.

Examples:

The use of the <u>Myers Briggs test</u> in <u>work teams</u>

The relationship between <u>parent training</u> and <u>school achievement</u> in <u>elementary school children</u>

<u>Predicting school achievement</u> in <u>grade school children</u>

Impact of <u>teacher expectations</u> on <u>achievement</u> in <u>high school students</u>

<u>Support</u> for <u>caregivers</u> of <u>Alzheimer's patients</u>

<u>Develop a list of search terms for each concept and determine in which fields to search them</u>
Most subject information is found in the following fields:

Title

Descriptor

Key Phrase

Abstract

Table of Contents

Information about the population and its geographical location is found in separate fields:

Population

Population Age

Population Location.

Locate *Thesaurus* terms for each concept. The most efficient starting place to find subject terms for your search is the *Thesaurus of Psychological Index Terms, the list of controlled vocabulary used to index each item in PsycINFO. Most search systems offer an electronic Thesaurus* with PsycINFO so you can search for terms and click to enter them in your search. The *Thesaurus* is also available in printed form and may be found in your library or purchased from the American Psychological Association.

Permuted and hierarchical listings of *Thesaurus* terms: Use the permuted display (each term alphabetized by every word in the term) to find a likely descriptor for your topic. Then look it up in the hierarchical display to see whether there are narrower or related terms that might also be used in your search. If all of the narrower terms are relevant, select them all or "explode" the main term. "Exploding" means searching the main term and all its narrower terms at once. If you see a +, arrow, or [NT] next to a narrower term, it tells you that this term also has narrower terms. Go to that term's hierarchy and, if the narrower terms are relevant, select them or explode the new main term.

Scope Note. There is other useful information in the electronic and paper *Thesaurus* listing: the year the term began, a scope note with usage information, and sometimes information about earlier terms used for this concept. Sometimes you find that the term has only been used for a few years; in that case, you should consider free-text searching in addition to *Thesaurus* term searching.

Mapping concepts to relevant index terms. *Thesaurus* terms can be located in other ways. If your search system has a mapping or suggest utility, you can enter a word or phrase in the search box and request that it be mapped. The system will present you with a list of *Thesaurus* terms that have been assigned frequently to the records in which your phrase occurred. Pick relevant terms from the list and, enter them in your search. If you have a *Thesaurus*, find out when they began and whether there are relevant related or narrower terms.

Pearl-growing search. Lacking a *Thesaurus* and a mapping/suggest utility, there is a third way you can find relevant terms. Perform a free-text search in the title and key phrase and display the descriptor field. When you find a relevant article, look at the descriptors. If there is one that covers your concept, enter it in your search.

Example:

A search of "sibling conflict" yields terms SIBLING RELATIONS, SIBLINGS, CONFLICT, and CONFLICT RESOLUTION.

Entering SIBLING* in the descriptor field and CONFLICT in the descriptor field results in more retrieval than the phrase by itself.

Note: The historic portion of PsycINFO and PsycLIT (1887-1966) does not contain a descriptor field. These records were created before there was a *Thesaurus*. Therefore, any search on descriptors will automatically limit your search to 1967 and later.

Search concepts with no *Thesaurus* terms free-text

If, after trying all of the techniques above, you still do not find any controlled vocabulary terms, you can search for occurrences of various words and phrases that you can think of for your concept. The prime fields for free-text searching are the title and key phrase. If you aren't finding many occurrences in these fields, you can extend the search to the abstract and the table of contents (for books).

You need to know the truncation symbols for your search system, so you can search stems for word variations.

Example:

famil* will retrieve family, families, familial, as well as familiar and familiarity

Some systems provide different functions for truncation symbols, for example, unlimited truncation vs. truncation limited to a specified number of characters.

When searching free-text, you must put yourself in the place of an author and think of as many different words and phrases as you can for a concept. Look at your retrieval-- you may find other terminology to feed back into your query.

For instance, if you search "five factor" for the five factor model of personality structure, you will soon see occurrences of "big five," as well. Adding that phrase and substituting the arabic 5 in both search statements will add many hundreds of records to the search.

It is important to know how your search system handles phrases. In most cases a phrase is searched as it is entered. However, some search systems insert "and" between the words, leading you to get less relevant results. In these cases, you can usually specify that the words should be searched as a phrase by inserting "adj" or putting the phrase in quotes.

<u>Searching for names as subjects.</u>

A limited number of personal, test, and drug names are found in the *Thesaurus* controlled vocabulary. Other names may be searched free-text in the Title, Key Phrase, Abstract, and Table of Contents.

<u>Personal names</u>. These are entered in first initial, last name format. Some names may be entered as just the surname (Hitler). Consider truncating the name as well (Nixon*, Freud*) to retrieve adjectival forms and possessives (Freudian, Nixon's).

<u>Test names</u>. Use the least number of words possible for test names leaving off such words as "survey, test, questionnaire," unless essential to differentiate from other tests, e.g., search *role construct repertory*, not *role construct repertory* test.

<u>Drug names</u>. Generic names are used to represent drugs in PsycINFO. Brand names retrieve few, if any, records.

Add terms from the population fields to your search scheme.

<u>Age groups</u>: Choices are Childhood, Neonatal, Infancy, Preschool Age, School Age, Adolescence, Adulthood, Young Adulthood, Thirties, Middle Age, Aged, and Very Old. Search one or more of the age groups on the accompanying list and combine the results with your search retrieval using AND.

<u>Population</u>: Choices are Human, Animal, Male, Female, Inpatient, Outpatient. It is surprising sometimes how much a search can be improved by merely limiting to a human population. For instance, if you want to know about the efficacy of a drug for humans, you may not want to see the animal research.

Likewise, if your interest is <u>women in sports</u>, you can do the search on athletes and limit the results to a female population. Since population categories are assigned each time they occur, many articles will be identified by both male and female population tags. To retrieve just female athletes, you must NOT [mark] out MALE in the population field.

Search example:

(athlet* or sports) in descriptors and female in population not male in population

<u>Population location</u>: If your search topic has a geographical element, and you are only interested in populations in certain countries, use the population location field.

Most search systems allow you to select population terms from a picklist or an index.

<u>Combine the terms for each concept</u>
When you have developed a list of *Thesaurus* terms and/or free-text phrases for each concept, combine them in a search statement inserting OR between them. OR broadens your search— retrieves items that have any one of the listed search terms.

Repeat this process for all concepts in your search.

<u>Combine the concepts</u>
When you have finished combining the terms for each concept, join the set numbers by entering them and inserting AND between them. This targets your search retrieval to items that have all concepts in them.

<u>View the records and refine the search</u>
Look at several records from the final search set (preferably samples from the beginning, middle, and end of the set) to see if they appear relevant. Here are some techniques for improving the relevance or the number of records found.

Not enough records:

Remove a concept from your strategy and re-run it.

If you're using free-text, see if you can find additional terms to search or use truncation to find more word variations.

Expand your title-key phrase search to the abstract and table of contents.

If you have received very few records and have not succeeded in broadening the search, consider whether another database might yield more citations.

Too many records:

Add another concept that will narrow your search to the particular aspect that you want.

Restrict your search to shorter, more relevant fields, such as title and key phrase.

Use positional operators, such as *near* and *with* rather than *and* in a free-text search.

Use limit fields to restrict the retrieval to desired document types or years of publication.

TABLE 3: EXAMPLE OF PsycINFO ABSTRACT FOR JOURNAL ARTICLE

Accession Number

Journal Article: 1997-38405-001.

Author

Vye, Nancy J; Goldman, Susan R; Voss, James F; Hmelo, Cindy; Williams, Susan.

Institution

Vanderbilt U, Learning Technology Ctr, Nashville, TN, USA.

Corporate/Institutional Author

Vanderbilt U, Cognition & Technology Group, Nashville, TN, USA

Title

Complex mathematical problem solving by individuals and dyads.

Source

Cognition & Instruction. Vol 15(4), 1997, 435-484.

ISSN

0737-0008

Language

English

Abstract

Reports the results of using a technique developed for analyzing complex problem solving: solution space analysis. The challenge is to construct a business plan for a booth at a school fun-fair fund-raiser. *[abstract continues]*

Key Phrase Identifiers

complex mathematical problem solving, individual 6th graders vs college students vs dyads of 5th graders

Subject Headings

*Age Differences *Dyads *Group Problem Solving *Mathematics *Problem Solving Adulthood Childhood School Age Children

Classification Code

Cognitive & Perceptual Development [2820]

Population Group

Human. Childhood (birth-12 yrs); School Age (6-12 yrs); Adulthood (18 yrs & older).

Population Location

USA

Form/Content Type

Empirical Study.

Special Feature

References.

Publication Type

Journal Article

Publication Year

1997

Update Code

19980401

TOPIC 5: ARCHIVAL RESEARCH

The laboratory goal for Topic 5 is to provide you with experience in carrying out archival research.

Behavioral scientists do not always work directly with participants. Much important information can be gathered indirectly through the study of records. There are many types of manipulations which cannot be imposed on individuals due to their ethical and/or procedural constraints. We cannot (and would not want to) impose natural disasters, job change, or death on individuals. Yet, records can let us study, retrospectively, a number of interesting behaviors.

Recorded information, both numerical and verbal, about individuals can provide rich information to investigate a variety of research questions. Statistical records are kept relating to many variables: (a) socioeconomic information, such as age, family size, and residence; (b) health statistics, such as birth and death rates; (c) public and private statistics, such as wages, hours of work, and financial transactions; and so on. Statistical records can be used as social indicators. Other archival sources are public or personal written documents: presidential talks, Congressional records, letters, diaries, school compositions, and so on. Another type of archival source is mass communications: magazines, newspapers, television, radio, videos, and the Internet.

LABORATORY EXERCISE 1: VIOLENCE IN MEDIA PROGRAMS

The purpose of this laboratory exercise is to provide you with experience in performing a content analysis of verbal and physical violence portrayed on television or in other media programs.

American children and adolescents spend an average of 3-5 hours per day with television, radio, videos, video games, and the Internet (Strasburger & Donnerstein, 2000). For some years behavioral scientists have been concerned whether observing media violence can increase viewers' aggressive behavior. While controversial, laboratory studies and some naturalistic studies tend to confirm a relationship between aggressive behavior and violent television (e.g., Asamen & Berry, 1998; Eron & Huesmann, 1987; Singer, Miller, Guo, Flannery, Frierson, & Slovak, 1999; Wiegman, Kuttschreuter, & Baarada, 1992) and video games (Dill & Dill, 1998). After reviewing research supporting and not supporting a link between viewing violence on television and in movies, Lande (1993) proposed there is a small group of vulnerable viewers. Television violence exposure, lack of parental monitoring, and television-viewing habits explained 45% of children's self-reported violent behaviors (Singer et al., 1999). Videotape violence increased aggression more so in high than low trait aggressive individuals (Bushman, 1995). Real-life violent game play was positively related to aggressive behavior and delinquency (Anderson & Dill, 2000).

Content analysis of 518 music videos broadcast over national music television networks during a 4-week period at randomly selected times of high adolescent viewership found the following: 14.7% portrayed overt interpersonal violence with a mean of 6.1 violent acts per violence-containing video, males were three times more likely to be aggressors, and attractive role models were aggressors in more than 80% of the violence (Rich, Woods, Goodman, Emans, & DuRant, 1998). The amount of violence portrayed varied significantly with the type of music: rap (20.4%), rock (19.8%), country (10.8%), adult contemporary (9.7%), and rhythm and blues (5.9%) (DuRant, Rich, Emans, Rome, Alfred, & Woods, 1997). Weapon carrying was higher in rock (19.8%) and rap (19.5%) videos.

TV content analysis research dealing with the prevalence of violence often concentrated upon physical violence (for a review, see Signorielli, Gross, & Morgan, 1982). Rates of five or six violent acts per hour on prime time TV was found in most countries (for review, see Cumberbatch, Jones, & Lee, 1988). Yet, violence may also be verbal in content. In a study of the portrayal of aggression on North American (U.S. and Canada) television, Williams, Zabrack, and Joy (1982) reported that an average of nine acts of physical aggression and 7.8 acts of verbal aggression per program hour were observed. Certain modes of aggression were more common than others. Physical aggression involving the body or a weapon accounted for 48.5% of all aggressive behavior observed. The proportion of acts using the other modes were as follows: physical threat, 9%; verbal threat, 18.25%; verbal abuse, 15%; sarcasm, 8.9%; political/socioeconomic, 0.9%; passive aggression/harassment, 1%; and symbolic/joking, 7.4%. Often aggression was portrayed as a successful means to resolve conflict.

Among other things, Williams et al. (1982) examined the overall violence mean ratings for various types of programs. They had coders rate the degree of violence (defined as "physical or psychological injury, hurt, or death" (p. 369)) on a scale from 1 (not at all violent) to 7 (very violent). The mean ratings for the various types of programs were the following: adventure programs, 3.6; animated programs (cartoons), 5.2; documentary programs, 4.6; drama and medical programs, 1.9; game programs, 1.0; instruction and religion programs, 1.8; music, variety, and talk programs, 2.2; and situation comedy programs, 2.8. These researchers concluded that there is much evidence for a link between television and viewers' beliefs about social reality. Their coders "agreed that 25% of the programs carried the message 'The world is a dangerous place to be.'" (p. 377). They used schema theory to help explain the impact television's content has on viewers' beliefs. As they noted,

> . . . A schema is a cognitive model (belief or concept) that is built up and modified as information is acquired. In general, its complexity will vary directly with the amount of relevant information and experience the individual acquires. Once a schema is established, it is used to process new information in what amounts to a matching process; the individual searches cognitively for a schema into which to fit information she or he encounters. . . . Schema theory would help to explain why adults' beliefs about social reality are most open to influence by television when they are not actively involved in viewing (Hawkins & Pingree, 1982). In the low involvement situation, a crude fit of the schema to incoming information will be acceptable, whereas high involvement will result in a more careful attempt to match, and viewers will be more likely to notice discrepancies between their real-world experience and television's model of social reality, thereby rejecting television's model. . . . Television's impact . . . is strongest when other sources of relevant information are lacking. It also would explain why the evidence concerning television's influence on beliefs about social reality is strongest for areas of social reality related to violence; violence abounds on TV, is presented with little variation, and most viewers have restricted experience with it (pp. 377-378).

Williams et al. (1982) did their content analyses in 1977. Since then there has continued to be pressure from certain lay groups and governmental officials upon television producers to reduce the amount of violence portrayed in their programs. Has it worked? To determine this, this laboratory exercise provides you with the opportunity to evaluate a selection of television programs using Williams et al.'s (1982) coding categories. As a class, decide which types of programs you will evaluate (e.g., adventure, children's animated or non-animated, crime, documentary, drama, medical, or situation comedy programs). It is recommended that you choose a maximum of three program types. For instance, you might compare children's animated and non-animated programs, prime time comedy and non-comedy programs, or different types of music videos. After you have determined the type of programs you will evaluate, choose representative productions for each. Determine whether you will watch one or more examples of each particular program. If you have two classmates analyze the same program, then you can examine inter-rater reliability. Coders are usually trained extensively before carrying out the actual research so that they are highly reliable; we realize that this is not possible in the present laboratory exercise.

Use the following definition of physical violence, which Williams et al. used: "'The overt expression of physical force (with or without weapon) against self or other, compelling action against one's will on pain of being hurt or killed, or actually hurting or killing. Must be plausible and credible; no idle threats, verbal abuse, or comic gestures with no credible violent consequences. May be intentional or accidental; violent accidents, catastrophes, acts of nature are included' (Gerber, Note 1)" (p. 366). Aggression may also be verbal threats/abuse, passive aggression and harassment, sarcasm, or joking.

On the following page, tally the number of times you see each mode of aggression on the program. Also rate the overall violence of each program on a 7- point scale from 1 (not at all violent) to 7 (very violent). With your classmates, collapse your data within each program category. Determine the mean rate of acts per program hour for each of the modes of aggression. Determine the overall mean violence rating for each category. Your instructor will direct you as to how to analyze and write up this study. If you are interested in doing further research in this field, an excellent source is Asamen and Berry (1998). They provide concrete, step-by-step examples.

Television Violence References:

Anderson, C. A., & Dill, K. E. (2000). Video games and aggressive thoughts, feelings, and behavior in the laboratory and in life. *Journal of Personality and Social Psychology, 78,* 772-790.

Asamen, J. K., & Berry, G. L. (1998). *Research paradigms, television, and social behavior.* Thousand Oaks, CA: Sage Publications, Inc.

Bushman, B. J. (1995). Moderating role of trait aggressiveness in the effects of violent media on aggression. *Journal of Personality and Social Psychology, 69,* 950-960.

Cumberbatch, G., Jones, I., & Lee, M. (1988). Measuring violence on television. Special Issue: Violence on television. *Current Psychology Research and Reviews, 7,* 10-25.

Dill, K. E., & Dill, J. C. (1998). Video game violence: A review of the empirical literature. *Aggression and Violent Behavior, 3,* 407-428.

DuRant, R. H., Rich, M., Emans, S. J., Rome, E. S., Alfred, E., & Woods, E. R. (1997). Violence and weapon carrying in music videos. A content analysis. *Archives of Pediatric and Adolescent Medicine, 151,* 443-448.

Eron, L. D., & Huesmann, L. R. (1987). Television as a source of maltreatment of children. *School Psychology Review, 16,* 195-202.

Gerber, G. (1974). *Cultural indicators project: TV message analysis recording instrument (Rev. ed).* Philadelphia, PA: Annenberg School of Communications, University of Pennsylvania.

Lande, R. G. (1993). The video violence debate. *Hospital and Community Psychiatry, 44,* 347-351.

Rich, M., Woods, E. R., Goodman, E., Emans, S. J., & DuRant, R. H. (1998). Aggressors or victims: gender and race in music video violence. *Pediatrics, 101,* 669-674.

Signorelli, N., Gross, L., & Morgan, M. (1982). Violence in television programs: Ten years later. In *Television and behavior: Ten years of scientific progress and implications for the eighties (Vol. 2).* Rockville, MD: NIMH.

Singer, M. I., Miller, D. B., Guo, S., Flannery, D. K., Frierson, T., Slovak, K. (1999). Contributors to violent behavior among elementary and middle school children. *Pediatrics, 104,* 878-884.

Strasburger, V. C., & Donnerstein, E. (2000). Children, adolescents, and the media in the 21st century. *Adolescent Medicine, 11,* 51-68.

Wiegman, D., Kuttschreuter, M., & Baarda, B. (1992). A longitudinal study of the effects of television viewing on aggressive and prosocial behaviours. *British Journal of Social Psychology, 31,* 147-164.

Williams, T. M., Zabrack, M. L., & Joy, L. A. (1982). The portrayal of aggression on North American television. *Journal of Applied Social Psychology, 12,* 360-380.

Tally Sheet: Modes of Aggression on Television

	Program #1	Program #2	Program #3
Program Name			
Time/Date			
Length in Minutes			
Number of Acts Involving: 1. Violence to Body			
2. Use of Weapon			
3. Physical Threat			
4. Verbal Threat			
5. Sarcasm			
6. Passive Aggression, Harassment			
7. Symbolic/Joking			
Total Number of Aggressive Acts			
Overall Violence Rate: 1 (none) to 7 (very violent)			

LABORATORY EXERCISE 2: GRAFFITI

The purpose of this laboratory exercise is to provide you with experience in performing a content analysis of graffiti.

Graffiti are the anonymous inscriptions, markings and pictures on surfaces produced privately but often for later public observation and response by others. While many view graffiti as a nuisance and the result of vandalism or aberrant behavior (e.g., Mueller, Moore, Doggett, & Tingstrom, 2000), others see it as a way to communicate and pass on information. Thus, graffiti serve a variety of purposes: "to teach, to pass on information, to voice discontent and rebel, and to assert one's individuality" (Roscoe & Evans, 1986, p. 221). Its value as an unobtrusive measure of human thought is valued in social science (Klofas & Cutshall, 1985; Webb, Campbell, Schwartz, Sechrest, & Grove, 1981).

Anderson and Verplanck (1983) categorized western world graffiti into three primary categories: tourist graffiti, inner-city graffiti, and restroom graffiti. In old archeological ruins, such as Egyptian pyramids and Mayan buildings, as well as in contemporary buildings and on natural landmarks such as rocks and trees, one finds tourist graffiti: names, dates, expressions of love, and even statements. American inner-city graffiti take three major forms: (1) "the special language of the ghetto youth, which is largely concerned with names and identify, and is characterized by constructions such as the reflexive 'as', in 'Clarence as Lefty' or 'Lefty as Clarence'"; (2) gang graffiti, "which serve both to define one's 'turf' and to ward off interlopers"; and (3) the "graffiti 'masters', the 'kings of the walls,' whose names or logos, often in colored splendor, adorn buildings, subway cars stations, bridges, trucks -- even elephants and airplanes" (Anderson & Verplanck, 1983, p. 342). In recent years there has been an increase of "Hip Hop" graffitti ranging from signature tags to elaborate polychrome spray-painted murals that can be studied to learn about the writers' values (Brewer & Miller, 1990). The most common graffiti are found in public restrooms, but there is an increase in graffiti on city streets.

Graffiti in public restrooms may be quickly scrubbed away by the janitors or left; some bar owners even provide blackboards to encourage patrons to write only there and not vandalize the walls. In general, more graffiti are found in male than female restrooms. Female graffiti make fewer sexual references and are usually more socially acceptable in regard to language and content (Arluke, Kutakoff, & Levin, 1987; for review, see Anderson & Verplanck, 1983). Bruner and Kelso (1980) found restroom graffiti written by women to be more interpersonal, interactive and romantic, while men's graffiti tended to be more egocentric and contain more competitive statements about love.

While some research (e.g., Anderson & Verplanck, 1983) is atheoretical, much of the early research was driven by Freudian theory and interpreted graffiti in terms of unconscious impulses, primitive thoughts, and infantile sexuality. More recently, some researchers take the perspective that graffiti "reflect the power positions of men and women in the social structure" (Bruner & Kelso, 1980, p. 250). Coming from a cognitive developmental perspective, Lucca and Pacheco (1986) interpreted children's graffiti in Puerto Rican schools in terms of its relationship to "the child's immediate life experiences such as concerns with their self- identity, interpersonal relations, cultural understandings, sexuality, and religious and political beliefs" (p. 465). Graffiti can be indicators of individual's or group's social attitudes, such as towards war or homosexuality, and as such can show attitude differences of them on campuses or in different socioeconomic areas of a town.

Given this as a background, your laboratory assignment is to collect graffiti from restrooms, or other public places, on your campus and/or in your town. Decide which buildings and public places will be surveyed, and assign students to collect the graffiti.

Record all graffiti in each place selected. You may wish to determine if the graffito is a reply to a previously existing graffito. After the data have been collected, each graffito must be categorized by content or theme. In a study of restrooms at the University of Tennessee in 1980, Anderson and Verplanck (1983) employed the following categories (percentages found in their study are provided in parentheses): political statements or references to political candidates (18%); humorous statements that are not targeted (14%); simple replies to other graffito that differs in content (11%); references to sex (11%); references to race (8%); general insults that defame a group or individual (7%); references to music (6%); references to religion (6%); references to fraternities or sororities (5%); references to drugs (3%); references to sports (2%); references to nuclear power or environmental issues (2%); statements that are philosophical in tone (2%); and miscellaneous which was less than 1% in a category (5%). You may use these categories or develop your own.

Rater reliability can be determined by having two students independently categorize the graffiti, or a subset of them, and then determine the percent of agreement between the raters. Anderson and Verplanck (1983) reported a rater reliability (percentage agreement) of 92%; while quite adequate it was not higher because some raters were unfamiliar with certain names, music or political issues.

For the purpose of comparison, Chi-square tests of significance can be used to determine differences between (1) male and female restrooms; (2) restrooms in different buildings on campus (for example, humanities and arts compared with engineering); (3) restrooms in buildings in different areas of a city; and/or (4) restrooms in public places which provide different services (for example, college campus and bars downtown). You might also wish to compare your findings with previous ones published in the literature (e.g., Anderson & Verplanck, 1983; Arluke et al., 1987; Bruner & Kelso, 1980) so that you can provide a historical perspective. Your instructor will direct you as to how to write up this laboratory exercise.

Graffiti references:

Anderson, S. J., & Verplanck, W. S. (1983). When walls speak, what do they say? *Psychological Record, 3*, 341-359.
Arluke, A., Kutakoff, L., & Levin, J. (1987). Are the times changing? An analysis of gender differences in sexual graffiti? *Sex Roles, 16*, 1-7.
Brewer, D. D., & Miller, M. L. (1990). Bombing and burning: The social organization and values of Hip Hop graffiti and implications for policy. *Deviant Behavior, 11*, 345-369.
Bruner, E. M., & Kelso, J. P. (1980). Gender differences in graffiti: A semiotic perspective. *Women's Studies International Quarterly, 3*, 239-252.
Klofas, J. M., & Cutshall, C. R. (1985). The social archeology of a juvenile facility: Unobtrusive methods in the study of institutional cultures. Special Issue: Innovative sources and uses of qualitative data. *Qualitative Sociology, 8*, 368-387.
Lucca, N., & Pacheco, A. M. (1986). Children's graffiti: Visual communication from a developmental perspective. *Journal of Genetic Psychology, 147*, 465-479.
Mueller, M. M., Moore, J. W., Doggett, R. A., & Tingstrom, D. H. (2000). The effectiveness of contingency-specific and contingency-nonspecific prompts in controlling bathroom graffiti. *Journal of Applied Behavioral Analysis, 33*, 89-92.
Roscoe, B., & Evans, J. A. (1986). Desk top graffiti. *College Student Journal, 20*, 221-224.
Webb, E. J., Campbell, D. T., Schwartz, R. F., Sechrest, L., & Grove, J. B. (1981). *Nonreactive Measures in the Social Sciences*, 2nd Edition. Boston, MA: Houghton Mifflin.

TOPIC 6: SURVEYS

The laboratory goal for Topic 6 is to provide you with experience in evaluating published survey questionnaires, administering questionnaires, and analyzing and interpreting your questionnaire results. The first laboratory exercise requires you to evaluate published survey questionnaires. The subsequent exercises provide anonymous survey questionnaires which you may administer. Your instructor will assign the ones you are to complete.

It is essential that the responses to each survey remain completely anonymous. It is recommended that you stand away from your respondent while he or she fills out the questionnaire. Also have the respondent put the questionnaire into a manila envelope to insure anonymity.

LABORATORY EXERCISE 1: EVALUATING SURVEYS

The purpose of this laboratory exercise is to provide you with experience in evaluating published survey questionnaires.

Bring to class any questionnaire you can find. Some common sources include: (1) popular magazines, such as *Psychology Today, Time*, or *Newsweek*; (2) newspapers, either your local paper or a national paper such as *USA Today*; (3) a national census questionnaire that can be obtained in the U.S. Documents section of your library; or (4) a national poll done by a private pollster company, such as Gallop Poll. On the Internet you can find questionnaires. The American Psychological Society maintains a superb link to Internet research: http://psych.hanover.edu/APS/exponnet.html

As a class, or in small groups, evaluate your questionnaires as to possible biases in the questions and how well the questions are written. Were there any biases in the sampling procedures? If so, how might they influence the validity of the survey and the degree to which the results can be generalized to other populations? Were there any biases in the reporting of the results?

When you evaluate the questions themselves, ask the following:

1. Can the question be misunderstood? Is it too difficult for the less educated respondent?

2. Does the question assume too much knowledge upon the part of the respondent?

3. Is the question too long?

4. Does the question have double negatives?

5. Is the wording of the question biased or slanted towards a certain viewpoint?

6. Is the wording of the question leading? In other words, does it try to put words into the mouth of the respondent?

7. Is the best response format used? For instance, are enough alternatives provided if it is a fixed-alternative item. Or, would the question be better as a dichotomous response (e.g., true or false) or as a multiple-choice response (e.g., always, usually, sometimes, rarely, never)?

List below at least three biased and/or poorly written questions from the questionnaires you evaluated. Explain why each is biased or poorly written.

Rewrite the above questions so that they do not contain the flaws you identified.

LABORATORY EXERCISE 2: INTERNET SURVEY RESEARCH

The purpose of this laboratory exercise is to give you experience in taking and critiquing an Internet-based questionnaire.

The Internet provides us with a new avenue to access the general public as well as particular groups. Most psychological survey research has used paper-and-pencil questionnaires that required the researchers to input their data into the computer before analyses could be made. This was tedious and open to experimenter error. The advent of Internet-based questionnaires has advantages and disadvantages. "Transposition errors" are minimized or eliminated. Speed of inputting and analyzing the data is increased. Participants are individuals you never have direct contact with. You can have access to subgroups on your campus (e.g., introductory psychology students; all students hooked up to the Internet) or to individuals around the world. A major disadvantage is that your respondents must be connected to the computer. New biases in selection of respondents are present and often unknown. You do not have control over who responds to your questionnaire (and how often they do it), unless you have restricted access to the questionnaire through the use of a keyword or some other means.

Before you begin this laboratory exercise, you are encouraged to access at least one report on Internet research. Researchers Carver, Kingston, and Turton at the School of Geography, University of Leeds, England, provide an excellent report on "A review of graphical environments on the World Wide Web as a means of widening public participation in social science research" Their web site is http://www.ccg.leeds.ac.uk/agocg/report.htm#content. They give a detailed examination of five case study sites: psychology survey; review of web-based tools for creating questionnaires and inputting and analyzing survey results; landscape preferences; where to dispose of Britain's nuclear waste; and virtual reality.

Your task in the present laboratory exercise is to participate in an Internet-based questionnaire. One excellent source is the American Psychological Society's web site for links to surveys presently being conducted on the Internet: http://psych.hanover.edu/APS/exponnet.html. Another excellent source is Dr. Birnbaum's site "Psychological Experiments on the Internet". He has a recent book on the topic (Birnbaum, 2000). His web site is http://psych.fullerton.edu/mbirnbaum/web/IntroWeb.htm.

Either individually or as a class, choose a survey in which you wish to participate. First, participate as the respondent. Second, read any further information that may be provided by the researchers. Finally, critique the questionnaire (see questions in Lab Exercise 1) and discuss the pros and cons of this research approach, as well as your personal reactions to it. You may wish to download the questionnaire so that you can administer the questionnaire to your classmates and analyze the results.

If you wish to develop your own Internet-based questionnaire, Dr. Paul Kenyon, Department of Psychology, University of Plymouth, England, has an excellent site on the nuts and bolts of putting together an Internet questionnaire. He also gives you a crash course in using HyperText Markup Language (HTML). His web site is http://salmon.psy.plym.ac.uk/mscprm/forms.htm.

Internet References:

Birnbaum, M. H. (2000). *Psychological experiments on the Internet.* San Diego: Academic Press.

LABORATORY EXERCISE 3: SURVEY ON ALCOHOL USE

The purpose of this laboratory exercise is to give you experience in conducting a survey. You may wish to present a summary of your findings to your counseling or health center, or newspaper.

College students' alcohol consumption is a serious problem. From 85% to 95% of all college students drink alcohol (Presley, Meilman, & Lyerla, 1994; Wechsler, Fulop, Padilla, Lee, & Patrick, 1997). In both colleges and high schools, its prevalence is moderated by demographic variables (e.g., Skager & Fisher, 1989; Wechsler et al., 1997). Studies (e.g., Barnes, Welte, & Dintcheff, 1992; Haworth-Hoeppner, Globett, Stem, & Morasco,1989; Kraft, 1985; O'Hara, 1990) have found that similar percentages of college men and women report alcohol consumption, but that men continue to be more frequent and heavier users of alcohol. This may be due in part to women perceiving a greater risk with use of alcohol than men (Spigner, Hawkins, & Loren, 1993). One in five living in a fraternity or sorority were heavy drinkers in a recent university survey (Haworth-Hoeppner et al., 1989; see also Borsari & Carey, 1999). Alterman et al. (1990) reported that nearly half of their sample of college men experienced two or more drinking-related adverse consequences and over a third were intoxicated four or more times monthly within the past year. About 10% of college students reported that their parents have drinking problems, and 23% of these students met DSM-IV criteria for alcohol abuse (Weitzman & Wechsler, 2000).

Episodic or binge drinking is a very serious health problem among college students. Binge drinking is defined as "five or more drinks in a row for men and four or more for women, at least once in the 2 weeks preceding the survey" (Wechsler, Lee, Kuo, & Lee, 2000, p. 199). Two of five students (44%) were binge drinkers both in 1993 and 1999 surveys of over 14,000 students at 119 nationally representative 4-year colleges in 39 states. In 1999, both abstainers (19%) and frequent binge drinkers (23%) were more prevalent than in 1993. Video coverage of Dr. Wechsler's press conference on March 14, 2000, can be seen at http://www.hsph.harvard.edu/video/#wechsler. In another study of data from the Harvard School of Public Health College Alcohol Study (1993), Wechsler and his colleagues (Wechsler, Molnar, Davenport, & Baer, 1999) found that frequent binge drinkers drank a median of 14.5 drinks per week, whereas infrequent binge drinks drank 3.7 and non-binge drinkers drank 0.7 drinks.

Comparisons across studies can be confounded by differential indices for the categorization of alcohol drinking levels. Early researchers often depended upon frequency of alcohol use to define alcohol usage categories, while more recently often a combination of both frequency of use and the typical quantity of alcohol consumed at any one occasion is used. For instance, Haworth-Hoeppner et al. (1989) reported (p. 840) the following categories in their study of over 1,000 randomly chosen students at a moderately sized (15,000-16,000), state-supported Southern university:

Nondrinker: those who drink less than once a year or not at all
(total: 16%; men: 15%; women: 17%)

Infrequent: those who drink at least once a year, but less than once a month
(total: 10%; men: 7%; women: 12%)

Light: those who drink at least once a month, but no more than 1-3 drinks per occasion (total: 14%; men: 11%; Women: 17%)

Moderate: those who drink at least once a month with no more than 4-5 drinks, once or twice a week with 1-3 drinks per occasion, or 5 times per occasion, or 5 times a week with 1 or less drinks per occasion

	(total: 24%; men: 20%; women: 27%)
Moderate-Heavy:	those who drink at least once a month with 6+ drinks per occasion, once or twice a week with 4-5 drinks per occasion, 4 to 5 times a week with 2-3 drinks, or 4 times a week with 2-3 drinks, or 4 times a week with 4-5 drinks per occasion (total: 22%; men: 25%; women: 20%)
Heavy:	those who drink once or twice a week with 6+ drinks per occasion or 5 times a week with 4-5 drinks per occasion
	(total: 14%; men: 22%; women: 7%)

Complications accompanying alcohol usage increase substantially in moderate to heavy alcohol users (e.g., Alterman et al., 1990; Haworth-Hoeppner et al., 1989; Pang, Wells-Parker, & McMillen, 1989). In Table 1 are presented the percentages of college students who reported complications within the previous year in Haworth-Hoeppner et al.'s survey (1989).

In a survey of over 4,000 university students between 1986 and 1988, Gonzalez (1989) found that those participants "who started to drink in elementary and middle school reported significantly higher levels of consumption and problems than Ss who started drinking while in high school or college" (p. 225).

In another study (Alterman et al., 1989) of college men at a large private university in northeastern United States, 40% were categorized as problem drinkers (intoxicated 2 or more times per month and having suffered at least two adverse consequences within the past year), yet very few thought they had a problem. "The most commonly reported adverse consequences were: blackouts- 53%; missed time from school or work due to drinking- 41%; binges of two or more days- 23%; and the shakes- 21%" (p. 99). Sweeney (1989) provides a review of data about the alcohol- memory disturbance of blackouts, and how their relate to our current thinking about memory processes.

Other important areas of research assess the correlates of alcohol abuse and attitudes towards alcohol consumption. There are thousands of studies in the literature on either of these general topics. Their findings guide us in the development of laws, alcohol prevention programs, and therapeutic approaches to treating alcoholism.

Your task is to conduct a survey of alcohol usage and alcohol-related problems on your campus, using a questionnaire we developed (Crawford & Desiderato, 1995) that is based upon research by Haworth-Hoeppner et al. (1989) and others. Five copies are provided in Appendix A; you may make more copies. It is extremely important that the survey be anonymous and that you have received approval from your human subjects committee. Develop a preliminary statement that explains the survey, states who is conducting it, states it is completely anonymous, and explains how to return the survey so that it is treated anonymously. Your teacher and human subjects committee will provide your school's guidelines. In Topic 14, Laboratory Exercise 2, is a sample consent form for an anonymous survey that was conducted by Crawford's research methods class.

A number of hypotheses based upon prior studies can be investigated with the survey's data. You may develop your own hypotheses, as well as use the following:

1. An equal number of men and women will report drinking alcohol in the past year.
2. Men will report substantially heavier drinking patterns than women.

3. Those individuals who report moderate to heavy drinking patterns will report alcohol-related problems.
4. Those individuals who report early drinking ages will report more moderate to heavy drinking patterns than will those who started drinking at a later age.

The chi-square is an appropriate statistic to use to assess the above hypotheses. Note that you will need to determine how you will operationally define your categories of alcohol use. Your teacher will instruct you as to how to write up this survey study.

Alcohol References:

Alterman, A. I., Hall, J. G., Purteill, J. J., Serales, J. S., Holahan, J. M., & McLellan, A. T. (1990). Heavy drinking and its correlates in young men. *Addictive Behaviors, 15*, 95-103.

Barnes, G. M., Welte, J. W., & Dintcheff, B. (1992). Alcohol misuse among college students and other young adults: Findings from a general population study in New York State. *International Journal of the Addictions, 27*, 917-934.

Borsari, B. E., & Carey, K. B. (1999). Understanding fraternity drinking: five recurring themes in the literature, 1980-1998. *Journal of American College Health, 48*, 30-37.

Desiderato, L. & Crawford, H. J. (1995). Risky sexual behavior in college students: Relationships between number of sexual partners, disclosure of previous risky behavior, and alcohol use. *Journal of Youth and Adolescence, 24*, 55-68.

Gonzalez, G. M. (1989). Early onset of drinking as a predictor of alcohol consumption and alcohol-related problems in college. *Journal of Drug Education, 19*, 225-230.

Goodwin, L. (1992). Alcohol and drug use in fraternities and sororities. *Journal of Alcohol and Drug Education, 37*, 52-63.

Hanson, D. J., & Engs, R. C. (1986). Correlates of drinking problems among collegians. *College Student Journal, 20*, 141-146.

Haworth-Hoeppner, S., Globetti, G., Stem, J., & Morasco, F. (1989). The quantity and frequency of drinking among undergraduates at a Southern university. *International Journal of the Addictions, 24*, 829-857.

Kaplan, M. S. (1979). Patterns of alcoholic beverage use among college students. *Journal of Alcohol & Drug Education, 24*, 26-40.

O'Hare, T. M. (1990). Drinking in college: Consumption patterns, problems, sex differences. and legal drinking age. *Journal of Studies on Alcohol, 51*, 536-541.

Pang, M. G., Wells-Parker, E., & McMillan, D. L. (1989). Drinking reasons, drinking locations, and automobile accident involvement among collegians. *International Journal of the Addictions, 24*, 215-227.

Presley, C. A., Meilman, P. W., & Lyerla, R. (1994). Development of the core alcohol and dug survey: Initial findings and future directions. *Journal of American College Health, 42*, 248-255.

Skager, R., & Fisher, D. G. (1989). Substance use among high school students in relation to school characteristics. *Addictive Behaviors, 14*, 129-138.

Spigner, C., Hawkins, W., & Loren, W. (1993). Gender differences in the perception of risk associated with alcohol and drug use among college students. *Women Health, 20*, 87-97.

Sweeney, D. F. (1989). Alcohol versus Mnemosyne: Blackouts. *Journal of Substance Abuse Treatment, 6*, 159-162.

Wechsler, H., Fulop, M., Padilla, A., Lee, H., & Patrick, K. (1997). Binge drinking among college students: A comparison of California with other states. *Journal of American College Health, 45*, 273-277.

Wechsler, H., Lee, J. E., Kuo, M., & Lee, H. (2000). College binge drinking in the 1990s: A continuing problem. Results of the Harvard School of Public Health 1999 College Alcohol Study. *Journal of American College Health, 48*, 199-210.

Wechsler, H., Molnar, B. E., Davenport, A. E., & Baer, J. S. (1999). College alcohol use: A full or emty glass? *Journal of American College Health, 47*, 247-252.

Weitzman, E. R., & Wechsler, H. (2000). Alcohol use, abuse, and related problems among children of problem drinkers; findings from a national survey of college alcohol use. *Journal of Nervous and Mental Diseases, 188*, 148-154.

TABLE 1

Percentage of College Drinkers who have Complications*

Complications	Percentage of Drinker Types				
	Infrequent	Light	Moderate	Moderate-Heavy	Heavy
Had hangover	23	44	80	91	93
Nauseated/vomited	16	28	45	61	68
Driven after several drinks	22	37	66	87	89
Drunk while driving	12	21	47	74	81
Driven after knowing had too much to drink	22	37	66	87	89
Arrested DWI	1	2	2	3	7
Gone to class after several drinks	2	7	10	25	39
Missed class because of hangover	3	16	38	67	69
Criticized for drinking	6	6	13	18	23
Thought might have drinking problem	4	3	3	10	27
Got lower grade	1	7	7	14	25
Got into fight	2	5	9	18	25
Damaged property	2	3	11	13	27
Trouble with law	1	3	3	9	21

* Adapted from Haworth-Hoeppner et al., (1989, p. 848-849, Table 3) with permission from authors and by courtesy of Marcel Dekker Inc.

LABORATORY EXERCISE 3: SURVEY ON EATING DISORDERS

The purpose of this laboratory exercise is to give you experience in conducting and analyzing a survey regarding eating disorders. You may wish to present a summary of your findings to your counseling center, health center, Dean of Students, or student newspaper.

Both the public sector and various health disciplines have been concerned with the growing number of people who are experiencing eating disorders, namely anorexia nervosa and bulimia. They have become increasingly prevalent during the last decade. This is partially attributed to societal pressures to control one's weight (Streigel-Moore, Silberstein, & Robin, 1986) and social contagion (Crandall, 1988). Sometimes athletes may experience pressure to maintain certain weights that may lead to eating disorders (e.g., Johnson, Powers, & Dick, 1999; Smolak, Murnen, & Ruble, 2000). Prevalence estimates have ranged from 2% to over 18% in women (Thelen, McLaughlin-Mann, Pruitt, & Smith, 1987). While no longer rare, these eating disorders are more prevalent among normal-weight women than men. According to the American Psychiatric Association's (1994) *Diagnostic and Statistical Manual of Mental Disorders*, 4th edition (DSM-IV), there are two types of Anorexia Nervosa: restricting type and binge-eating/purging type. The DMS-IV diagnostic criteria of Anorexia Nervosa are

A. Refusal to maintain body weight at or above a minimally normal weight for age and height (e.g., weight loss leading to maintenance of body weight less than 85% of that expected; or failure to make expected weight gain during period of growth, leading to body weight less than 85% of that expected).
B. Intense fear of gaining weight or becoming fat, even though underweight.
C. Disturbance in the way in which one's body weight or shape is experienced, undue influence of body weight or shape on self-evaluation, or denial of the seriousness of the current low body weight.
D. In postmenarcheal females, amenorrhea, i.e., the absence of at least three consecutive menstrual cycles. (A woman is considered to have amenorrhea if her periods occur only following hormone, e.g., estrogen administration). (pp. 544-545)

There are two types of Bulimia Nervosa: purging type and nonpurging type. The DSM-IV diagnostic criteria of Bulimia Nervosa are

A. Recurrent episodes of binge eating. An episode of binge eating is characterized by both of the following:
   (1) eating, in a discrete period of time (e.g., within any 2-hour period), an amount of food that is definitely larger than most people would eat during a similar period of time and under similar circumstances
   (2) a sense of lack of control over eating during the episode (e.g., a feeling that one cannot stop eating or control what or how much one is eating)
B. Recurrent inappropriate compensatory behavior in order to prevent weight gain, such as self-induced vomiting; misuse of laxatives, diuretics, enemas, or other medications; fasting; or excessive exercise.
C. The binge eating and inappropriate compensatory behaviors both occur, on average, at least twice a week for 3 months.
D. Self-evaluation is unduly influenced by body shape and weight.
E. The disturbance does not occur exclusively during episodes of Anorexia Nervosa. (pp. 549-550)

Various self-report questionnaires have been devised to assess symptoms of these eating disorders and to identify abnormal eating patterns in college students (e.g., Hart & Ollendick, 1985; Joiner, Vohs, & Heatherton, 2000; Lundholm & Wolins, 1987), children and adults. The International Journal of Eating Disorders is one journal that is devoted to eating problem research. One excellent self-report questionnaire which assesses symptoms of bulimia is the BULIT (Smith & Thelen, 1984) or BULIT-R

(Thelen, Farmer, Wonderlich, & Smith, 1991; Welch, Thompson, & Hall, 1993).

Your task is to conduct a survey of a sample of students on your campus to determine the distribution of bulimia among men and women. You will use the BULIT-R. Five copies of the BULIT-R can be found in Appendix A. Eight unscored items have been removed from this version. If you need more copies, you have permission to make photocopies. In class, determine how your class can best randomly sample your campus. Your instructor will direct you as to how to write up this survey study.

In addition to examining percentages of responses to each of the categories between men and women, you could do further analyses by weighing the responses as Thelen et al. (1990) did. All BULIT-R items are present in a 5-point, forced choice Likert format. Five points are given for the extreme "bulimic" direction, down to one point for the extreme "normal" direction. Some items are reversed in order to prevent a response bias. Those items for which $a = 1$, $b = 2$, $c = 3$, $d = 4$, and $e = 5$ are: 1, 3, 4, 8, 16, 18, 20, 21, 26, and 27. Those items for which $a = 5$, $b = 4$, $c = 3$, $d = 2$, and $e = 1$ are: 2, 5, 6, 7, 9, 10, 11, 12, 13, 14, 15, 17, 19, 22, 23, 24, 25 and 28. Thelen et al. (1990) employ a cutoff of 104 or above to meet the scale criteria for bulimia, although they suggest lowering it to a cutoff of 85 to reduce the number of false negatives.

Eating Disorders References:

American Psychiatric Association. (1994). *Diagnostic and Statistical Manual of Mental Disorders* (Revised 4th ed). Washington, D.C.: American Psychiatric Association.

Brelsford, T. N., Hummel, R. M., & Barrios, B. A. (1992). The Bulimia Test - Revised: A psychometric investigation. *Psychological Assessment, 4,* 399-401.

Crandall, C. S. (1988). Social contagion of binge eating. *Journal of Personality and Social Psychology, 55,* 588-598.

Hart, K. J., & Ollendick, T. H. (1985). Prevalence of bulimia in working and university women. *American Journal of Psychiatry, 142,* 851-854.

Joiner, T.E. Jr, Vohs, K. D., & Heatherton, T. F. (2000). Three studies on the factorial distinctiveness of binge eating and bulimic symptoms among nonclinical men and women. *International Journal of Eating Disorders, 27,* 1980295.

Lundholm, J. K., & Wolins, L. (1987). Disordered eating and weight control behaviors among males and female university students. *Addictive Behaviors, 12,* 275-279.

Johnson, C., Powers, P.S., & Dick, R. (1999). Athletes and eating disorders: the National Collegiate Athletic Association study. *International Journal of Eating Disorders, 26,* 179-188.

Smith, M. C., & Thelen, M. H. (1984). Development and validation of a test for bulimia. *Journal of Consulting and Clinical Psychology, 52,* 863-872.

Smolak, L., Murnen, S. K., & Ruble, A. E. (2000). Female athletes and eating problems: a meta-analysis. *International Journal of Eating Disorders, 27,* 371-380.

Stein, D. M., & Brinza, S. R. (1989). Bulimia: Prevalence estimates in female junior high and high school students. *Journal of Clinical Child Psychology, 18,* 206-213.

Streigel-Moore, R. H., Silberstein, L. R., & Rodin, J. (1986). Toward an understanding of risk factors for bulimia. *American Psychologist, 41,* 246-263.

Thelen, M. H., Farmer, J., Wonderlich, S., & Smith, M. (1991). A revision of the Bulimia Test: the BULIT-R. *Psychological Assessments: A Journal of Consulting and Clinical Psychology, 3,* 119-124.

Thelen, M. H., McLaughlin-Mann, L. M., Pruitt, J., & Smith, M. (1987). Bulimia: Prevalence and component factors in college women. *Journal of Psychosomatic Research, 31,* 73-78.

Welch, G., Thompson, L., & Hall, A. (1993). The BULIT-R: Its reliability and clinical validity as a screening tool for DSM-III-R bulimia nervosa in a female tertiary education population. *International Journal of Eating Disorders, 14,* 95-105.

LABORATORY EXERCISE 4: SURVEY ON ESP ATTITUDES AND EXPERIENCES

The purpose of this laboratory exercise is to give you experience in conducting a survey, analyzing its results, and comparing the results to those in the literature.

The existence of extrasensory perception (ESP) has been the center of great controversy in the field of science. In one survey (Palmer, 1979) over half of a sample of college students and townspeople in Charlottesville, Virginia, and surrounding communities reported that they had at least one ESP experience. Many of the surveys about psychic experiences have been conducted on preselected samples or subsamples of the general population, such as college students. Others have attempted to obtain a more representative sample of the general population. Reports of having ESP experiences are, of course, not the same as demonstrating ESP under stringent laboratory controls. Yet, it is important to know how many people believe in ESP and how many people claim to have had ESP experiences, with a breakdown of various kinds.

Vitulli and his associates at the University of South Alabama used our survey on ESP attitudes and experiences in studies of college students in a course in experimental parapsychology (Vitulli, 1997) and of age and sex differences in paranormal beliefs among elderly persons and undergraduate students (Vitulli, Tipton, & Rowe, 1999). In the first study, Vitulli (1997) found no significant differences in paranormal beliefs before or after the course. The results showed that "belief in life after death, belief in the existence of extrasensory perception, and belief in precognitive experiences in dreams ranked highest in endorsement while beliefs in out-of-the-body experiences, auras, or psychokinesis, ranked lowest" (p. 273).

Your task is to conduct a survey of attitudes towards ESP and of reported ESP experiences. In Appendix A there are 5 copies of a questionnaire on ESP which the authors developed for your use. You may photocopy more copies, if needed, for your study.

In class determine the group of people you will sample. Determine how you will randomly sample this group and how many questionnaires each of you will distribute.

Once you have conducted your survey, determine how you will analyze the data. Percentages of men, women, and total sample who answered yes to each statement can be determined easily. On the next page a table for your data summary is provided. Compare your findings with other surveys listed below. Write up the laboratory exercise according to your instructor's directions.

References:

Alvarado, C. S. (1987). Observations of luminous phenomena around the human body: A review. *Journal of the Society for Psychical Research, 54*, 38-60.

Blackmore, S. J. (1984). A postal survey of OBEs and other experiences. *Journal of the Society for Psychical Research, 52*, 225-244.

Haraldsson, E. (1985). Representative national surveys of psychic phenomena: Iceland, Great Britain, Sweden, USA and Gallup's multinational survey. *Journal of the Society for Psychical Research, 53*, 145-158.

Johnson, R. D., & Jones, C. H. (1984). Attitudes towards the existence and scientific investigation of extrasensory perception. *Journal of Psychology, 117*, 19-22.

Palmer, J. (1979). A community mail survey of psychic experiences. *Journal of the American Society for Psychical Research, 73*, 221-251.

Rhine, L. E. (1956). Hallucinatory psi experiences. I. An introductory survey. *Journal of Parapsychology, 20*, 233-256.

Schmeidler, G. R. (1985). Belief and disbelief in psi. *Parapsychology Review, 16*, 1-4.

Vitulli, W. F. (1997). Beliefs in parapsychological events or experiences among college students in a course in experimental parapsychology. *Perceptual and Motor Skills, 85*, 273-274.

Vitulli, W. F., Tipton, S. M., & Rowe, J. L. (1999). Beliefs in the paranormal: age and sex differences among elderly persons and undergraduate students. *Psychological Reports, 85*, 847-855.

Table 1

Percentage of Respondents Claiming Belief in ESP or ESP Experiences

Statement		Men	Women	Total
BELIEFS				
in the existence of ESP	Yes			
	No			
ghosts exist	Yes			
	No			
life after death	Yes			
	No			
people can contact the dead	Yes			
	No			
flying saucers and people from other planets	Yes			
	No			
EXPERIENCES				
had an ESP experience	Yes			
	No			
telepathic experience	Yes			
	No			
precognitive dream	Yes			
	No			
out-of-body experience	Yes			
	No			
have seen a ghost	Yes			
	No			
experienced psychokinesis	Yes			
	No			
seen an aura	Yes			
	No			

TOPIC 7: EX POST FACTO STUDIES

The laboratory goal for Topic 7 is to provide you with experience in evaluating and conducting ex post facto studies. Ex post facto means "after the fact". In ex post facto studies the researcher is interested in the effects of previously determined traits, behaviors, or naturally occurring events on subsequent performance, attitudes, etc. The antecedent conditions can be genetically determined groups (e.g., birth disorder, sex), personality groups (e.g., introverts and extroverts), mental disorders (e.g., paranoid vs nonparanoid schizophrenics), life event conditions (e.g., divorced or raped), and so on.

The crucial point is that the antecedent condition cannot or should not be manipulated by the researcher. An ex post facto study looks like a true experiment but it is not since the researcher did not manipulate the antecedent conditions. Unlike a true experiment, there is no random assignment of participants to conditions. The preexisting differences are the "manipulation", and the researcher is interested in the effect of these differences on subsequently measured variables. In addition, no conclusions of cause and effect can be made because some other variable other than that which was manipulated may have caused the relationship. Yet, like correlational studies, we can examine relationships between variables and learn much important information about correlates of preexisting individual differences.

LABORATORY EXERCISE 1: EVALUATING EX POST FACTO STUDIES

The purpose of this laboratory exercise is to provide you with experience in evaluating abstracts from published ex post facto studies. Your instructor may wish you to read one or more of these studies. Here your task is to identify (a) the groups, and subgroups, of participants who were studied and on what criteria they were chosen, (b) the variables that were measured, (c) the results that were reported, and (d) any alternative factors, other than those studied, that may have contributed to the identified relationships. On a sheet of paper, write your answers for each selection and turn them into your instructor at the assigned time.

Barton, R. A., & Whiten, A. (1993). Feeding competition among female olive baboons, Papio anubis. *Animal Behaviour, 46,* 777-789.

Competition for food is thought to play a key role in the social organization of group-living primates, leading to the prediction that individual foraging success will be partly regulated by dominance relationships. Among adult females in a group of free-ranging olive baboons, dominance rank was significantly correlated with nutrient acquisition rates (feeding rates and daily intakes), but not with dietary diversity or quality, nor with activity budgets. The mean daily food intake of the three highest-ranking females was 30% greater than that of the three lowest-ranking females, providing an explanation for relationships between female rank and fertility found in a number of other studies of group-living primates. The intensity of feeding competition, as measured by supplant rates and spatial clustering of individuals, increased during the dry season, a period of low food availability, seemingly because foods eaten then were more clumped in distribution than those eaten in the wet season. Implications for models of female social structure and maximum group size are discussed.

Christensen, L., & Somers, S. (1996). Comparison of nutrient intake among depressed and nondepressed individuals. *International Journal of Eating Disorders, 20*, 105-109.

OBJECTIVE: The study investigated the nutrient intake of depressed and nondepressed subjects. METHOD: Twenty-nine depressed subjects and a matched group of nondepressed subjects completed a 3-day food record. RESULTS: Results revealed that depressed and nondepressed groups consume similar amounts of all nutrients except protein and carbohydrates. Nondepressed subjects consume more protein and depressed subjects consume more carbohydrates. The increase in carbohydrate consumption comes primarily from an increase in sucrose consumption. DISCUSSION: The increased carbohydrate consumption is consistent with the carbohydrate cravings characteristic of the depressed and may related to the development or maintenance of depression.

Crawford, H. J., Brown, A. M., & Moon, C. (1993). Sustained attentional and disattentional abilities: Differences between low and highly hypnotizable persons. *Journal of Abnormal Psychology, 102*, 534-543.

Relations between sustained attentional and disattentional abilities and hypnotic susceptibility (Harvard Group Scale of Hypnotic Susceptibility: Form A; Stanford Hypnotic Susceptibility Scale: Form C) were examined in 38 low (0-3) and 39 highly (10-12) hypnotizable college students. Highs showed greater sustained attention on Necker cube and autokinetic movement tasks and self-reported greater absorption (Tellegen Absorption Scale) and extremely focused attentional (Differential Attentional Processes Inventory) styles. Hypnotizability was unrelated to dichotic selective attention (A. Karlin, 1979) and random number generation (C. Graham & F. J. Evans, 1977) tasks. Discriminant analysis correlated classified 74% of the lows and 69% of the highs. Results support H. J. Crawford and J. H. Gruzelier's (1992) neuropsychophysiological model of hypnosis that proposes that highly hypnotizable persons have a more efficient far frontolimbic sustained attentional and disattentional system.

Winokur, G., Coryell, W., Endicott, J., & Akiskal, H. (1993). Further distinctions between manic-depressive illness (bipolar disorder) and primary depressive disorder (unipolar depression). *American Journal of Psychiatry, 150*, 1176-1181.

Objective: Patients with bipolar disorder differ from patients with unipolar depression by having family histories of mania with an earlier onset and by having more episodes over a lifetime. This study was designed to determine whether additional aspects of course of illness, the presence of medical diseases, childhood traits, and other familial illnesses separate the two groups. Method: In a large collaborative study, consecutively admitted bipolar and unipolar patients were systematically given clinical interviews. Data were collected on medical diseases and childhood behavioral traits. Systematic family history and family study data were also obtained. The patients were studied every 6 months for 5 years. Results: The group of bipolar patients had an earlier onset, a more acute onset, more total episodes, and more familial mania and were more likely to be male. These differences were relatively independent of each other.

Winocur, G. (1990). A comparison of cognitive function in community-dwelling and institutionalized old people of normal intelligence. *Canadian Journal of Psychology, 44*, 435-444.

Two carefully matched groups of normal old people living in institutions or in the community were administered a neuropsychological cognitive test battery. In general, the institutionalized group performed worse than the community group. Discriminant function analysis identified a subgroup of high-functioning institutionalized subjects whose performance more closely resembled that of the community group than the remainder of the institutionalized group. Differences between the various groups were not due to differences in IQ, age, health, or other controlled variables. The critical tests that differentiated the groups were sensitive to impaired function in frontal and medial-temporal lobe brain regions. The results suggest a complex interaction involving effects of age and environmental factors on brain function and cognition.

LABORATORY EXERCISE 2: GENDER DIFFERENCES IN SPATIAL ABILITY

The purpose of this laboratory exercise is to teach you how to do ex post facto research.

Before proceeding to read the material presented in this laboratory, your instructor will give you a timed visuospatial test that will be found in Appendix B. **DO NOT LOOK AT THE TEST UNTIL YOUR INSTRUCTOR DIRECTS YOU!** As a class, read together the instructions and then do the sample problems. Your instructor will time you on the two parts of the test; each part takes 3 minutes. When you have completed the test, score it.

Male advantage for a variety of spatial ability tasks has been reported extensively, yet some meta-analyses (e.g., Caplan, MacPherson, & Tobin, 1985; Hyde, 1981) have suggested that such a conclusion is unwarranted because the proportion of variance accounted for by gender differences is less than 5%. When examined more closely, substantial and quite consistent gender differences occur on tasks requiring the manipulation of three-dimensional objects (e.g., Collins & Kimura, 1998; Linn & Petersen, 1985; Masters, 1998; Vandenburg & Kuse, 1979). The relationship between hormonal levels and visuospatial performance has been investigated. In men, testosterone level may play a moderating role on performance (Silverman, Kastuk, Choi, & Phillips, 1999). In women, performance changes across the menstrual cycle are inconsistently observed (Epting & Overman, 1998; Moody, 1997). Both environmental and genetic factors, in a complex interplay at different times and in different combinations, contribute to spatial ability development (Ashton & Borecki, 1987; Casey, Nuttall, & Pezaris, 1999; Goldstein, Haldane, & Mitchel, 1990; Vandenberg & Kuse, 1979).

In this laboratory exercise, you have just taken the Mental Rotations Test (Vandenberg & Kuse, 1978). There is consistent evidence in the literature that men perform significantly better than women on this test (e.g., Collins & Kimura; Masters, 1998; Geary, Gilger, & Elliott-Miller, 1992; Masters & Sanders, 1993; Vandenberg & Kuse, 1979). Your task is to determine whether there are significant gender differences on the Mental Rotations Test for your class.

Your instructor will inform you as to how to do a t-test for independent groups and direct you as to how to write up this study.

In addition, discuss how these differences might have come about. Do your parents have similar visuospatial abilities? As a child did you have a lot of experience manipulating things (e.g., puzzles, climbing trees, etc.)? What strategies did you use while you were doing the test (visualizing holistically vs verbalizing the parts)?

If you have a large enough sample, you may wish to investigate whether there is a relationship between visuospatial performance and menstrual cycle in women. For this, you will need to review the literature quoted above to determine how to operationally define menstrual phase and luteal phase, and to address individual differences in menstrual cycles. In Topic 9, Laboratory Exercise 2 (Production of Visual Illusion Reversals - Practice Effects), it is suggested that you could correlate Mental Rotation Test performance with number of reversals reported for the Necker Cube and Schroder Staircase reversal figures.

Spatial References:

Ashton, G. C., & Borecki, I. B. (1987). Further evidence for a gene influencing spatial ability. *Behavioral Genetics, 17,* 243-256.

Caplan, P.7 J., MacPherson, G. M., & Tobin, P. (1985). Do sex-related differences in spatial abilities exist? A multilevel critique with new data. *American Psychologist, 40,* 786-799.

Casey, M. B., Nuttall, R. L., & Pezaris, E. (1999). Evidence in support of a model that predicts how biological and environmental factors interact to influence spatial skills. *Developmental Psychology, 35,* 1237-1247.

Collins, D. W., & Kimura, D. (1997). A large sex difference on a two-dimensional mental rotation task. *Behavioral Neuroscience, 111,* 845-849.

Epting, L. K., & Overman, W. H. (1998). Sex-sensitive tasks in men and women: a search for performance fluctuations across the menstrual cycle. *Behavioral Neuroscience, 112,* 1304-1317.

Geary, D. C., Gilger, J. W., & Elliott-Miller, B. (1992). Gender differences in three-dimensional mental rotation: A replication. *Journal of Genetic Psychology, 153,* 115-117.

Goldstein, D., Haldane, D., & Mitchell, C. (1990). Sex differences in visual-spatial ability: The role of performance factors. *Memory and Cognition, 183,* 546-550.

Hyde, J. S. (1981). How large are cognitive gender differences? A meta-analysis using W^2 and D. *American Psychologist, 36,* 892-301.

Linn, M.A., & Petersen, A. C. (1985). Emergence and characterization of sex differences in spatial ability: A meta-analysis. *Child Development, 56,* 1479-1498.

Maccoby, E. M., & Jacklin, C. N. (1974). *The psychology of sex differences.* Stanford, CA; Stanford University Press.

Masters, M. S. (1998). The gender difference on the Mental Rotations test is not due to performance factors. *Memory and Cognition, 26,* 444-448.

Masters, M. S., & Sanders, B. (1993). Is the gender difference in mental rotation disappearing? *Behavioral Genetics, 23,* 337-341.

Moody, M. S. (1997). Changes in scores on the Mental Rotations Test during the menstrual cycle. *Perceptual and Motor Skills, 84,* 955-961.

Silverman, I., Kastuk, D., Choi, J., & Phillips, K. (1999). Testosterone levels and spatial ability in men. *Psychoneuroendocrinology, 24,* 813-822.

Vandenberg, S., & Kuse, A. R. (1978). Mental rotations: A group test of three-dimensional spatial visualization. *Perceptual and Motor Skills, 47,* 599-604.

Vandenberg, S., Kuse, A. R. (1979). Spatial ability: A critical review of the sex-linked major gene hypothesis. In M. Wittig & A. C. Petersen (Eds.), *Sex-related differences in cognitive functioning,* (pp. 67-95). New York: Academic Press.

SCORING FORM: MENTAL ROTATIONS TEST

For the Mental Rotations Test (Vandenberg & Kuse, 1978), use the following scoring instructions to determine your score after taking the test in class. The following scoring key presents each item and the possible four response figures. The two that are correct in each line are in boxes. Circle those figures which you correctly identified and put an X through those figures which you incorrectly identified. Do not evaluate any figure that you did not answer. In other words, we are only interested in the number of correctly marked figures and the number of incorrectly marked figures.

Part 1:

1. [1] 2 [3] 4
2. [1] 2 3 [4]
3. 1 [2] 3 [4]
4. 1 [2] [3] 4
5. [1] 2 [3] 4
6. [1] 2 3 [4]
7. 1 [2] 3 [4]
8. 1 [2] [3] 4
9. 1 [2] 3 [4]
10. [1] 2 3 [4]

Part 2:

11. 1 [2] 3 [4]
12. 1 [2] 3 [4]
13. 1 [2] 3 [4]
14. [1] 2 3 [4]
15. 1 [2] 3 [4]
16. 1 [2] [3] 4
17. [1] 2 [3] 4
18. [1] 2 3 [4]
19. 1 [2] 3 [4]
20. 1 [2] [3] 4

Determine how many correct and incorrect figures you identified. Remember not to include items which you did not answer.

	Part 1:	Part 2:	Parts 1 and 2 together:
correct:	____	____	____
incorrect:	____	____	____

Often cognitive tests take off for guessing by subtracting a certain percentage of the number wrong from the number right. For each problem, there are four possible answers, but only two are correct. The probability is that random responses would have given you a 50% chance of being correct (2 out of 4). Therefore, to correct for guessing, you are to subtract 1/2 of the number wrong from the number right. Calculate the corrected total score for Parts 1 and 2, separately and together.

Part 1:	Part 2:	Parts 1 and 2 together:
____	____	____

Do a mixed factor analysis of variance to determine if there main effects for gender (independent groups) and part (repeated measures), as well as an interaction effect.

LABORATORY EXERCISE 2: ASSIGNING PARTICIPANTS TO TREATMENT GROUPS

The purpose of this laboratory exercise is to give you practice in using various methods to assign participants to treatment groups.

A graduate student in sports psychology at the University of Missouri proposed to answer this research question as part of her Master's thesis: What are the effects of viewing Olympic swimmers' training films on subsequent swimming skills?

In order to recruit participants, she put a notice on the sign-up board asking for participants who were nonswimmers (had never learned to swim) and interested in learning how to swim. Slots were open for a total of 40 participants: 20 men and 20 women. Participants were told to report at the same designated time to the women's gymnasium. At that time participants were to be assigned to two "classes" of swimming training:

Class 1: Participants would watch films of Olympic swimmers' training sessions before actually going into the pool for lessons.

Class 2: Participants would go straight into the pool for lessons without seeing the films.

The dependent variable was "swimming ability". This was measured in two ways: (1) the obtained score on a short swimming skills knowledge test, and (2) the actual distance the participant could swim across the shallow end of the Olympic sized pool after a one hour training session.

The graduate student assigned participants to the two classes on the basis of when they showed up for the session. The first 20 were assigned to Class #1 and the second 20 were assigned to Class #2. As can be seen in Table I, this selection procedure caused some potential problems: the participants were not evenly matched. In Table I, the participants are listed in the order in which they arrived. Their gender, weights, and IQs are also reported. As you can see, more women than men were the first to show up. In Class #I there were 6 men and 14 women, while in Class #2 there were 14 men and 6 women. Secondly, the mean weights of the two groups were significantly different: respectively, 135.2 and 149.95. Finally, the mean IQs were different: respectively, 111.2 and 103. Reflect for a moment as to why these differences might have occurred. These variables could possibly affect swimming ability. They are extraneous variables which need to be controlled.

Your task is to employ more appropriate "selection" procedures to form the two treatment groups ("classes") so that they are better equated on the variables under question. Specifically, you are to assign the participants in Table 1 to the two groups, using each of the following three methods:

1. Random Assignment

2. Matching by precision control for (a) gender, (b) gender and weight, and (c) gender, weight, and IQ.

3. Matching building gender into the design.

Indepth information about these three methods are provided below.

METHOD 1: Straight Randomization

This technique is based on the premise that each participant has an equal chance of being selected for either experimental group (Class 1 or 2) in question. There are many ways this could be done. Here are two suggested ways.

A. Odd-Even Method
1. Go to a random numbers table, either in the Appendix of your experimental methods book or one provided by your instructor. Start anywhere you want in the table.
2. Reading one digit numbers in any direction, assign a random digit to each of the participants in the pool (in this case, 1 - 40).
3. Make up a rule for randomization. In this case, participants who have been assigned even numbers (0, 2, 4, 6, 8) will be place in treatment group 1, and those assigned odd numbers (1, 3, 5, 7, 9) will be placed in treatment group 2.
4. Once either group has been filled (20 participants in this case) then whatever participants are left over are assigned to the other group.

B. Direct Method
1. Go to a random numbers table. Start anywhere you want in the table.
2. Start running your finger in any direction looking for either a 1 (group 1) or a 2 (group 2). As soon as you come to a 1 or a 2, make the first participant go into that group.
3. Continuing from where you left off, again look for a 1 or a 2 for the second participant, and assign according to the number that comes up first (1 or 2).
4. Continue this way for all 40 participants.
5. As soon as one group fills up, all other participants must be placed in the unfilled group.

Whichever method is used, compare the characteristics of the randomly assigned groups to the groups selected by the graduate student. Answer the following:

1. How many males and females are in each of your groups?
2. What is the mean weight in each group?
3. What is the mean IQ in each group?

METHOD 2: Matching by Precision Control

If you wish to make absolutely sure that some of the traits are exactly equal in both groups, one approach you can take is matching by precision control.

A. Equating gender in each group
1. Go down the participant list. You find that the first participant is female.
2. Find another female to match the first female.
3. Assign one of these paired females to Group 1 and the other to Group 2, in a random fashion. Mark off each assigned female from your participant list.
4. Continue in this manner for the rest of the female participants.
5. Now do the same thing for the male participants, remembering to randomly assign the paired males to the two groups.

Now, check your groups. How many males and females are in each group? Have you used all 40 participants?

B. Equating gender and weight in each group

1. Find the first participant and note this participant's "values" on the variables under consideration: gender and weight. As you will note, the first participant is female and weighs 107 pounds.
2. You are now to find another participant who matches this participant on gender and weight. If there is a perfect match, randomly assign these two participants to the two groups. If there is no match, the first participant cannot be used and must be thrown out of the sample.
3. Continue in this manner for all 40 participants. Remember to cross off participants after they are assigned or thrown out.

Check your groups. How many participants are in each group? How many males and females are in each group? What are their average weights? Did you use all participants?

C. Equating gender, weight, and IQ in each group

Follow the same procedure as given above with all three variables. How many total participants are used? What are the limitations of Methods B and C when you match by precision control?

METHOD 3: Matching by Building into Design

If you think a variable (such as gender, weight, and/or IQ) could have a significant effect on swimming ability, you can examine that effect along with the effect of the training film by matching and building these variables into your design. Matching by building a variable into the design will allow you to determine if that variable will have any effect.

If you wished to determine the effect of gender, as well as the film, on swimming ability, you would do the following:

1. Separate the males and females into two separate groups.
2. Randomly assign all males to groups 1 and 2.
3. Randomly assign all females to treatment groups 1 and 2.

Such an assignment would result in four treatment groups, which could be graphed in the following manner.

TREATMENT GROUPS

		Class #1	Class #2
	Males	1	1
		.	.
		.	.
		n	n
GENDER			
	Females	1	1
		.	.
		.	.
		n	n

113

TABLE 1

Participants Listed in Chronological Order of Arrival

Name	Gender	Weight	IQ
First Twenty:			
1. Anna KannaFanna	F	109	110
2. Anita Newface	F	121	133
3. June Bugg	F	138	109
4. Wilbur Milburn	M	148	113
5. Illia Gitamate	F	136	101
6. Sam Dunkshot	M	195	148
7. Rick Shaw	M	185	130
8. Emma Knate	F	122	104
9. Ethyl Chloride	F	122	115
10. Mike Rofone	M	160	110
11. Fran Ennolly	F	113	122
12. Maye B. Knot	F	123	98
13. Jane Mundane	F	111	101
14. Polly Ester	F	134	120
15. I. C. Cream	M	167	94
16. Dee Leerious	F	147	96
17. Bob Frapples	M	152	112
18. Patti Kayck	F	105	100
19. Elenor Frozenfelt	F	120	103
20. Valerie Valerah	F	98	105
Second Twenty:			
21. Hal Itosis	M	163	82
22. Will Yadooit	M	180	110
23. Cora Lation	F	105	91
24. U. B. Trippin	M	167	106
25. Gail Warning	F	123	95
26. Barry A. Bone	M	210	117
27. Norm L. Curve	M	121	98
28. A. C. Deesey	M	135	102
29. Sharon Chairelyke	F	110	109
30. Oscar Meyer	M	139	131
31. Nick L. Beer	M	135	107
32. Buster Jaw	M	148	103
33. Jesse Minnitt	F	156	83
34. Cal Yafornia	M	178	112
35. Lena Onmie	F	119	85
36. Miles Standoffish	M	182	107
37. Elliot Mess	M	173	110
38. Rich O'Shay	M	152	105
39. Clara Nett	F	136	101
40. Johnny Stench	M	167	106

TOPIC 11: DESIGN

Topic 11 is concerned with the design of experiments. Several exercises will be provided to give you practice in actually designing experiments. Different research topics will be presented and your task will be to read the introductory material that describes the basic nature of the problem and then to design a study that investigates a component of this problem area. Since the introductory material will present only a brief introduction to the problem area, you would ordinarily not have sufficient knowledge to design an adequate experiment. To attempt to eliminate or at least minimize this deficit a variety of independent and dependent variables will be presented along with a typical procedure or procedures. Your task is to design a study using one or more of the independent and dependent variables specified. Your instructor will assign some or all of these exercises.

LABORATORY EXERCISE 1: DESIGNING AN OBESITY STUDY

During the past decade a great deal of scientific attention has been focused on the identification of factors relating to obesity. Within the general population, however, a dominant interest has naturally existed among those who are overweight. The overweight population seems to be continually seeking means for losing weight by means of one diet plan or another. Weight plans have proliferated, some of which have become faddish and captivated the interest of the overweight population. These weight reducing programs have been largely ineffective, judged by the fact that they do not enable the overweight person to reduce to and maintain a normal weight. A number of factors influence a person's food intake and weight gain. Research is directed toward the identification of these factors.

In the past, physiological psychologists have been interested in identifying the portion of the brain that controls eating behavior. Since such studies typically involve creating brain lesions, these studies are naturally not conducted on humans but on infrahumans such as rats, cats, and monkeys. These studies have found that bilateral lesions in the ventromedial nuclei of the hypothalamus will generally produce an animal that will eat prodigious amounts of food, producing a tremendous weight gain. The classic description of such an animal is that immediately following the operation, the animal staggers over to the food tray and begins voracious eating, which lasts for several weeks. Naturally there is an accompanying weight gain, which is labeled the "dynamic phase" of hyperphagia. Following this rapid weight gain a plateau is reached, the "static phase," at which point the animal's weight levels off and food intake drops to a level only slightly greater than that of the normal animal. During these two phases the lesioned animal remains inactive but emotional and irascible.

Such evidence would tend to suggest that a portion of the brain controls our eating behavior and maybe, in obese people, this control mechanism may have malfunctioned. However, other data suggest that there may be more involved. For example, if quinine is added to the food of a lesioned rat its food intake drops dramatically.

When turning to research on human participants, we find additional suggestive data. In an early studies, Stunkard and Koch (1964) found that there was little relationship between gastric motility and self-report of hunger in obese persons whereas this relationship did exist in the normal participant. Such evidence indicates that the obese person does not label bodily states associated with food deprivation as hunger, whereas the normal person does. Such evidence suggests that there must be other factors that determine whether or not the obese person will ingest food. Mood and affect are important ones (Christensen, 1993, 1997). Your task is to design a study which investigates these other variables.

In designing this study assume the following setting:

All participants are requested to report at the laboratory at 7:00 p.m. You had previously contacted them and asked them not to eat their evening meal prior to participating in the experiment. When the participant appears for the experiment you escorted him or her to a table and told the participant that you were conducting a study on taste.

Participants are then presented with several kinds of crackers, almonds, or types of sandwiches and are asked to taste each kind and rate them on a rating scale. Participants are also told to taste as many or as few crackers, almonds, or sandwiches of each type as they need in making their judgements. The important thing is that their rating be as accurate as possible.

Methodological Consideration

The primary consideration is the definition and measurement of obesity. As in the prior section dealing with independent variables, one must establish some criteria of what represents an obese person and what represents a normal person. This boils down to translating obesity into concrete operational terms. The most commonly used measures are as follows:

(1) Metropolitan Life Insurance tables of ideal or desired weight. Participants are classified as obese if their weight deviates by 15% or more over what the tables labeled as the ideal or desired weights.

(2) Triceps skin fold thickness measurements. This is a measurement which determines the amount of subcutaneous fatty tissue in the body. This latter measure is perhaps better since it has been shown to be independent of the height or frame of the individual. A person's tricep skin-fold thickness is compared to a distribution of such scores (Seltzer and Mayer, 1965). In the past at least one study has classified obese people as individuals whose scores fell in the fourth quartile while participants whose scores fell in the second quartile were classified as normal.

Possible Independent Variables

(1) Emotional Arousal - The psychosomatic hypothesis of obesity postulates that the obese eat in an attempt to cope with anxiety. In the laboratory this anxiety arousal could be created by threat of electrical shock.

(2) Food Cue Prominence - Schachter and his colleagues have emphasized the importance of seeing food. In other words, if food is highly visible it will operate as a cue to generate eating behavior. Therefore, to vary this variable one must conceive a way of varying the degree to which food cues are prominent as varying illumination or having the food wrapped.

(3) Taste - It has previously been found that rats with bilateral lesions in the ventromedial nuclei of the hypothalamus, after they have reached the static phase, will reduce their intake of food if it is laced with quinine. This suggests that taste may be a factor in the amount of food which is ingested by the obese. Therefore, to test the possibility of such a factor also affecting the behavior of humans one must vary the taste of the food given.

(4) Effort - It is possible that the obese, because they are heavier, may be less inclined to work for food than would their normal weight counterparts. To test this hypothesis it would be necessary to vary the difficulty in attaining the food.

(5) Gender - It is possible that male and female obese individuals respond differently in their eating patterns.

(6) Age - Obese children may respond differently than obese juveniles or obese adults.

<u>Dependent Variable</u>

In studies of obesity there is one primary dependent variable -- the amount eaten, whether it is number of crackers, nuts, or sandwiches, etc.

<u>Laboratory Exercise 1: Design of the Research</u>

Now that you have read the brief introductory material on obesity you are to conceptualize one or more research studies, to be specified by your instructor, that investigate one or more of the variables that have been specified. To accomplish this, you are to complete the following steps which correspond to steps that would actually be taken in the design of a study. Your instructor will go over these steps with you. Write it up on a separate sheet of paper and hand it into your instructor.

STEP 1. First Research Study: You are to first specify your research question and your scientific and null hypotheses.

Research question:

Scientific hypothesis:

Null hypothesis:

STEP 2. Design Specification: Now that you have specified your research question and your hypothesized outcome, you are to design an experiment that investigates this research using the APA Publication Manual guidelines.

Participants:

Materials:

Procedure:

References on Obesity:

Abramson, E. E., & Wunderlich, R. A. (1972). Anxiety, fear and eating: A test of the psychosomatic concept of obesity. *Journal of Abnormal Psychology, 79*, 317-321.

Andrews, H. B., & Jones, S. (1990). Eating behaviour in obese women: A test of two hypotheses. *Australian Psychologist, 25*, 351-357.

Bartlett, S. J., Faith, M. S., Fontaine, K. R., Cheskin, L. J., & Allison, D. B. (1999). Is the prevalence of successful weight loss and maintenance higher in the general community than the research clinic? *Obesity Research, 7*, 407-413.

Bowen, D. J., & Grunberg, N. E. (1987). Contributions of social psychology to the study of appetitive behaviors. *Journal of Applied Social Psychology, 17*, 622-640.

Christensen, L. (1993). Effects of eating behavior on mood: A review of the literature. *International Journal of Eating Disorders, 14*, 171-183.

Christensen, L. (1997). The effects of carbohydrates on affect. *Nutrition, 13*, 503-514.

Donnelly, J. E., Jacobsen, D. J., Heelan, K. S., Seip, R., & Smith, S. (2000). The effects of 18 months of intermittent vs continuous exercise on aerobic capacity, body weight and composition, and metabolic fitness in previously sedentary, moderately obese females. *International Journal of Obesity Related Metabolism Disorders, 24*, 566-572.

Drewnowski, A., Kurth, C., Holden-Wiltse, J., & Saari, J. (1992). Food preferences in human obesity: carbohydrates versus fats. *Appetite, 18*, 207-221.

Ganley, R. M. (1989). Emotion and eating in obesity: A review of the literature. *International Journal of Eating Disorders, 8*, 343-361.

Leon, G. R., & Chamberlain, K. (1973). Comparison of daily eating habits and emotional state of overweight persons successful or unsuccessful in maintaining weight loss. *Journal of Consulting and Clinical Psychology, 41*, 108-115.

McKenna, R. J. (1972). Some effects of anxiety level and food cues on the eating behavior of obese and normal subjects: A comparison of the Schachterian and psychosomatic conceptions. *Journal of Personality and Social Psychology, 22*, 311-319.

Nisbett, R. E., & Gurwitz, S. B. (1970). Weight, sex, and the eating behavior of human newborns. *Journal of Comparative and Physiological Psychology, 73*, 245-253.

Reisenzein, R. (1983). The Schachter theory of emotion: Two decades later. *Psychological Bulletin, 94*, 239-264.

Rodin, J. (1981). Current status of the internal-external hypothesis for obesity. What went wrong? *American Psychologist, 36*, 361-372.

Rodin, J., Elias, M., Silver stein, L. R., & Wagner, A. (1988). Combined behavioral and pharmacologic treatment for obesity: Predictors of successful weight maintenance. *Journal of Consulting and Clinical Psychology, 56*. 399-404.

Rzewnicki, R., & Forgays, D. G. (1987). Recidivism and self-cure of smoking and obesity: An attempt to replicate. *American Psychologist, 42*, 97-100.

Sarwer, D. B., & Wadden, T. A. (1999). The treatment of obesity: what's new, what's recommended. *Journal of Women's Health Gender Based Medicine, 8*, 483-493.

Schachter, S. (1971). Some extraordinary facts about obese humans and rats. *American Psychologist, 26*, 129-144.

Schachter, S., Goldman, R., & Gordon, A. (1968). Effects of fear, food deprivation, and obesity on eating. *Journal of Personality and Social Psychology, 10*, 91-97.

Singh, D. (1973). Role of response habits and cognitive factors in determination of behavior of obese humans. *Journal of Personality and Social Psychology, 27*, 220-238.

Spiegel, T. A., Shrager, E. E., & Stellar, E. (1989). Responses of lean and obese subjects to preloads, deprivation, and palatability. *Appetite, 13*, 45-69.

Stringel-Moore, R. H., Schreiber, G. B., Lo, A., Crawford, P., Obarzanek, E., & Rodin, J. (2000). Eating disorder symptoms in a cohort of 11 to 16-year-old black and white girls: the NHLBI growth and health study. *International Journal of Eating Disorders, 27*, 49-66.

LABORATORY EXERCISE 2: DESIGNING AN INTERPERSONAL ATTRACTION STUDY

As we go through our everyday lives we encounter many people whom we like or to whom we are attracted. By the same token we encounter some people whom we dislike. Interpersonal attraction, therefore, refers to the evaluation of another person in a positive or negative way. Explanations for why we become attracted to certain individuals but not to others has been the focus of attention and discussion for centuries. The issue of attraction has been the focus of systematic research in psychology and sociology.

One may ask why it is important to study attraction? While many reasons can be given, such as its relationship to other social problems as marital failure, the primary objective of researchers investigating interpersonal attraction is much more basic. Interpersonal attraction is investigated in an attempt to identify the processes and empirical laws that operate to generate a positive or negative evaluation of others.

Interpersonal attraction was virtually an untouched research area until Moreno (1934) developed the sociometric technique. With his development of sociometry, serious attention was paid to the topic because now a method had been developed that would allow one to obtain some measure of attraction. Since Moreno's sociometric technique required each member of a group to specify with which other member or members he or she preferred to associate, investigators researched the variables that were related to one's popularity in groups. More recently other approaches have dominated the field. The development of these additional approaches has been necessary to provide further impetus to the exploration of attraction. One of the paradigms that has been developed is Byrne's (1971) attraction paradigm. Attention will be focused on this approach since it has been extremely successful in enabling investigators to research a variety of antecedent issues which have increased our knowledge of the conditions surrounding attraction.

The attraction paradigm, which is advocated by Byrne, is a reinforcement paradigm or a conditioning model. Byrne proposed that any stimulus with reinforcement properties could function as an unconditioned stimulus in producing an affective response or a response following along the pleasant-unpleasant continuum. Any discriminable stimulus, such as a person, that is temporally associated with this unconditioned stimulus would then be conditioned to evoke the same implicit affective response as did the unconditioned stimulus. Since Byrne and his colleagues demonstrated that attitude statements can operate as unconditioned stimuli eliciting either positive or negative affective responses, a person (CS) who is associated with positive or negative attitudes (UCS) would through conditioning come to also elicit these positive or negative affective responses. Since these affective responses mediate evaluative responses such as like, dislike, and hate, a person would, according to Byrne and his colleagues, come to like or dislike another based on the attitudes he or she associated with that person.

To investigate the validity of this paradigm, Byrne and his colleagues devised the following procedures: During the first part of the semester participants are given the Survey of Attitudes (a 56-item attitude scale, developed in the 1960s, located at the end of this exercise). These participants are then randomly assigned to the designated experimental groups. A second bogus stranger then supposedly has taken the same attitude scale. This bogus stranger's responses are patterned by the experimenter so they will be similar or dissimilar to those expressed by the participant. There are several different ways in which these fake patterns of responses can be generated. Table 1 illustrates the possible method that can be used.

Table 1: Different Faking Patterns for Similar and Dissimilar Item Responses by Bogus Strangers[1]

Subjects' Responses	Identity -	Mirror	Moderate	Discrepancy	Constant	Discrepancy
	Similar	Dissimilar	Similar	Dissimilar	Similar	Dissimilar
1	1	6	2	5	2	4
2	2	5	3	4	1 or 3	5
3	3	4	2	5	2	6
4	4	3	5	2	5	1
5	5	2	4	3	4 or 6	2
6	6	1	5	2	5	3

[1]From Bryne, D. (1969). Attitudes and attraction. In L. Berkowitz (ed.), Advances in Experimental Social Psychology. New York: Academic Press.

Consequently, if you wanted to use the moderate discrepancy pattern in creating a similar bogus participant you would identify the participant's response (e.g., 4) and locate it in the first column. Then move across this row until you reach the moderate discrepancy/similar column. The number in that column (5) would represent the bogus participant's response. This procedure would be followed until you had provided a response for all items in the bogus participant's Survey of Attitudes scale. The actual participant's Survey of Attitudes scale along with his or her paired bogus participant's scale would then be returned to the participant with the following instructions. (The background information section is cut off with a scissors. Also participants are to complete the Interpersonal Judgement Scale after forming an opinion of the bogus person since this represents the dependent variable measure).

Earlier this semester, you filled out an attitude questionnaire called the Survey of Attitudes which dealt with a series of issues. One purpose was to learn something about student attitudes, but a second purpose was to determine the extent to which one person can form valid judgements about another person just by knowing a few of his attitudes. Last semester we carried out other studies of this sort. Students wrote down several sorts of information about themselves, their names were removed, and this information was given to other students. The task was to form an opinion about the stranger's intelligence, knowledge of current events, morality, and adjustment just on the basis of knowing a few bits of information about the person's past and present life. We found that students could guess these things with better than chance accuracy. So, this study is an extension of the previous one, and a major change has been introduced. Instead of information about the other person's life, you will be shown his or her attitudes on 26 specific issues. The background information was removed from each of these scales. Each of you will receive the attitude scale of another student. All I can guarantee is that this person is the same sex as yourself, to the best of our knowledge you do not know the person whose attitude scale you will receive, and it is not someone in the same psychology class as yourself. Please read the person's answers carefully and try to form an opinion about him or her. As soon as you have studied each of the attitudes, fill out the Interpersonal Judgement Scale and indicate your best guess as to this person's intelligence, knowledge of current events, morality, and adjustment. Also, indicate how much you think you would like to work with this person as partners in an experiment (Bryne, 1971, p. 51).

Possible Independent Variables

A. Proportion of Similar Attitudes. Since Byrne and his colleagues have advocated that positive attitudes elicit positive affective responses such as liking, a logical extension of this is that the greater the proportion of similar attitudes expressed by the bogus stranger, the greater the expressed liking for that stranger. To test the possibility one would have to vary the proportion of similar attitudes expressed by the bogus stranger to various groups of participants.

B. Topic Importance. One of the issues which can be raised when one discusses the attitude attraction field is the issue of the importance of the topic on which participants agree or disagree. It could be hypothesized that agreement or disagreement on important topics leads to greater liking or disliking than does agreement or disagreement on unimportant items. To investigate this possibility the items in the 56 item attitude scale must first be scaled for importance. Fortunately this has already been accomplished, allowing this hypothesis to be tested. The 14 most important items are items 5, 6, 10, 14, 17, 19, 25, 27, 31, 33, 34, 43, 46, 48. The next most important items are 12, 21, 45, 52, 55, 28, 22, 39, 51, 40, 3, 35, 56, 24; the 14 next-to-least important items are 53, 47, 8, 42, 13,

23, 16, 30, 44, 7, 29, 18, 1, 41; and the 14 least important items are 9, 50, 32, 15, 54, 37, 26, 36, 4, 38, 2, 11, 49, 20.

C. Sequential Presentation of Attitudinal Stimuli. In the field of impression formation one area of active research is on the impact of first impressions. This research has revealed that first impressions are often inaccurate and that we revise them as we continue interaction. A similar hypothesis could be stated about the relationship between attitudes and attraction. In most interpersonal encounters one hears attitudes and opinions that are both similar and dissimilar to one's own. Does the order in which these similar and dissimilar attitudes appear influence one's attraction?

D. Prestige or Status of the Bogus Stranger. In our daily encounter with others we come across others who exhibit greater or lesser prestige in our eyes. Prior sociometric studies have reported a positive relationship between prestige and friendship choices. One could then ask if this prestige factor operated over and above attitude similarity in producing attraction. If it did, then attraction from a high prestige person should be greater than that expected from a member of a peer group. In this context one might also inquire as to the effects generated by a prestigious person exhibiting attitude dissimilarity. It is very possible that such a person could elicit the greatest negative impact. Prestige could be altered by attributing to the bogus stranger a given occupational status, military rank, etc.

E. Gender. This is an obvious variable; however, it is one that may produce an interaction. For example, it is possible that similarity in attitude is more important in forming friendships with individuals of the same gender. Opposite-gendered friendships may be less dependent upon attitude similarity but more dependent upon factors such as physical attractiveness.

F. Emotional Disturbance. Byrne's reinforcement paradigm reveals hypotheses that attitude similarity should lead to attraction. However, what would be the relationship if the other or bogus stranger possessed attributes that were undesirable to us, such as emotional disturbance? Would such an undesirable attribute operate to reduce the effectiveness of attitude similarity? It is possible that it might since an attribute would make similarity unpleasant or even threatening.

G. Race. It has been suggested in the literature that racial prejudice is actually reducible to an assumption that individuals of a different race possess different beliefs. If this is so, then knowledge of belief similarity should override any racial prejudice that would exist. Within the Byrne paradigm it should be possible to determine if racial prejudice is a function of race or belief similarity.

Dependent Variable

Although there are a variety of dependent variables that have been identified for use in attraction research, the one that is consistently identified and used with the Byrne Attraction Paradigm is contained within the Interpersonal Judgement Scale (located at the end of this exercise). Although this scale requires each person to rate the bogus stranger on 7 items, only two of these items are used for assessment of attraction. These two items, "Would you like or dislike this person?" and, "Would you like or dislike working with this person?" are summed to provide a single measure of attraction ranging from a score of 2 (most negative) to a score of 14 (most positive). These two items are embedded in the context of the other 5 items to give the instructions concerning interpersonal judgement credibility.

Laboratory Exercise 2: Design of the Experiment

Now that you have read the introductory material concerning attraction, as well as the potential independent variables that could be used, you are to construct one or more research studies (to be specified by your laboratory instructor) that would investigate one or more of the specified independent variables. To accomplish this you are to complete the following steps.

STEP 1. First Research Study: You are to first specify your research question and your scientific or null hypothesis.

Research question:

Scientific hypothesis:

Null hypothesis:

STEP 2. Design Specification: Now that you have specified your research question and your hypothesized outcome, you are to design an experiment that investigates this research question using the APA Publication Manual guidelines.

Participants:

Materials:

Procedure:

References on Attraction:

Byrne, D. (1969). Attitudes and attraction. In L. Berkowitz (Ed.), *Advances in Experimental Social Psychology*. New York: Academic Press, Vol. 5.

Byrne, D. (1971). *The Attraction Paradigm*. New York: Academic Press.

Condon, J. W., & Crano, W. D. (1988). Inferred evaluation and the relation between attitude similarity and interpersonal attraction. *Journal of Personality and Social Psychology, 54*, 789-797.

Duck, S. (Ed.) (1977). *Theory and Practice in Interpersonal Attraction*. New York: Academic Press.

Griffin, E., & Sparks, G. G. (1990). Friends forever: A longitudinal exploration of intimacy in same-sex friends and platonic pairs. *Journal of Social and Personal Relationships, 7*, 29-46.

Grover, S. L., & Brockner, J. (1989). Empathy and the relationship between attitudinal similarity and attraction. *Journal of Research in Personality, 23*, 469-479.

Jamieson, D. W., Lyndon, J. E., & Zanna, M. P. (1987). Attitude and activity preference similarity: Differential bases of interpersonal attraction for low and high self-monitors. Special Issue: Integrating personality and social psychology. *Journal of Personality and Social Psychology, 53*, 1052-1060.

Smeaton, G., Byrne, D., & Murnen, S. K. (1989). The repulsion hypothesis revisited: Similarity irrelevance or dissimilarity bias? *Journal of Personality and Social Psychology, 56*, 54-59.

Now that you have designed an experiment in Laboratory Exercise 2, your instructor will select one of the proposed experiments to be conduced using the class as participants. The experimenter will be the student whose design has been selected. The primary criteria for selection will be adequacy of the design and its ability to be used within the context of the class. In carrying out the study, most of you will be participants. However, you are not naive in the same way as most participants are since you have read a little about interpersonal attraction and you designed a study related to it. Therefore, when participating as a participant you are going to have to role play and act as much like a naive participant as you can. This is extremely necessary for the data to be as uncontaminated as possible.

Experiment Proper. Your student experimenter and instructor will instruct you in the tasks you are to complete in your capacity as a participant. The Attitude Scale and Interpersonal Judgment Scale are provided on subsequent pages.[2]

Data Analysis. Now that you have served as a participant you are to obtain the data and analyze it as though you were the experimenter. Your instructor will give you the data in addition to explaining the design of the experiment. At this point you must ask any questions you think are necessary to clarify the experiment and to insure that you know what the experiment was attempting to accomplish. To assist in this regard you should record the research question null or scientific hypothesis. Once you have laid out your design you can record the raw data in the appropriate categories.

Research question:

Null hypothesis:

Scientific hypothesis:

Now that you have the raw data you are to analyze the data with the help of your laboratory instructor. When you complete the statistical analysis you are to write up the results as close as possible to APA format. Additional information on the APA format can be obtained from your experimental psychology textbook or from the APA *Publication Manual*.

---

[2]D. Byrne, *Attraction Paradigm,* pp. 416-427. New York: Academic Press, 1971, with permission.

Fifty-Six Item Attitude Scale

Survey of Attitudes

Name: _____ Psy.: _____ Sec.: _____ Date: _____

Age: _____ Sex: _____ Class: Fr. _____ Soph. _____ Jr. _____ Sr. _____

Hometown: _____

1. Fraternities and Sororities (check one)

_____ I am very much against fraternities and sororities as they usually function.
_____ I am against fraternities and sororities as they usually function.
_____ To a slight degree, I am against fraternities and sororities as they usually function.
_____ To a slight degree, I am in favor of fraternities and sororities as they usually function.
_____ I am in favor of fraternities and sororities as they usually function.
_____ I am very much in favor of fraternities and sororities as they usually function.

2. Western Movies and Television (check one)

_____ I enjoy western movies and television programs very much.
_____ I enjoy western movies and television programs.
_____ I enjoy western movies and television programs to a slight degree.
_____ I dislike western movies and television programs to a slight degree.
_____ I dislike western movies and television programs.
_____ I dislike western movies and television programs very much.

3. Undergraduates Getting Married (check one)

_____ In general, I am very much in favor of undergraduates getting married.
_____ In general, I am in favor of undergraduates getting married.
_____ In general, I am mildly in favor of undergraduates getting married.
_____ In general, I am mildly against undergraduates getting married.
_____ In general, I am against undergraduates getting married.
_____ In general, I am very much against undergraduates getting married.

4. Situation Comedies (check one)

_____ I dislike situation comedies very much.
_____ I dislike situation comedies.
_____ I dislike situation comedies to a slight degree.
_____ I enjoy situation comedies to a slight degree.
_____ I enjoy situation comedies.
_____ I enjoy situation comedies very much.

5. Belief in God (check one)

_____ I strongly believe that there is a God.
_____ I believe that there is a God.
_____ I feel that perhaps there is a God.
_____ I feel that perhaps there is no God.
_____ I believe that there is no God.
_____ I strongly believe that there is no God.

6. Professors and Student Needs (check one)

_____ I feel that university professors are completely indifferent to student needs.
_____ I feel that university professors are indifferent to student needs.
_____ I feel that university professors are slightly indifferent to student needs.
_____ I feel that university professors are slightly concerned about student needs.
_____ I feel that university professors are concerned about student needs.
_____ I feel that university professors are very much concerned about student needs.

7. Draft (check one)

_____ I am very much in favor of the draft.
_____ I am in favor of the draft.
_____ I am mildly in favor of the draft.
_____ I am mildly opposed to the draft.
_____ I am opposed to the draft.
_____ I am very much opposed to the draft.

8. Necking and Petting (check one)

_____ In general, I am very much against necking and petting among couples in college.
_____ In general, I am against necking and petting among couples in college.
_____ In general, I am mildly against necking and petting among couples in college.
_____ In general, I am mildly in favor of necking and petting among couples in college.
_____ In general, I am in favor of necking and petting among couples in college.
_____ In general, I am very much in favor of necking and petting among couples in college.

9. Smoking (check one)

_____ In general, I am very much in favor of smoking.
_____ In general, I am in favor of smoking.
_____ In general, I am mildly in favor of smoking.
_____ In general, I am mildly against smoking.
_____ In general, I am against smoking.
_____ In general, I am very much against smoking.

10. Integration in Public Schools (check one)

_____ Racial integration in public schools is a mistake, and I am very much against it.
_____ Racial integration in public schools is a mistake, and I am against it.
_____ Racial integration in public schools is a good plan, and I am mildly against it.
_____ Racial integration in public schools is a good plan, and I am mildly in favor of it.
_____ Racial integration in public schools is a good plan, and I am in favor of it.
_____ Racial integration in public schools is a good plan, and I am very much in favor of it.

11. **Comedians Who Use Satire** (check one)

_____ I very much enjoy comedians who use satire.
_____ I enjoy comedians who use satire.
_____ I mildly enjoy comedians who use satire.
_____ I mildly dislike comedians who use satire.
_____ I dislike comedians who use satire.
_____ I very much dislike comedians who use satire.

12. **Acting on Impulse vs. Careful Consideration of Alternatives** (check one)

_____ I feel that it is better if people always act on impulse.
_____ I feel that it is better if people usually act on impulse.
_____ I feel that it is better if people often act on impulse.
_____ I feel that it is better if people often engage in a careful consideration of alternatives.
_____ I feel that it is better if people usually engage in a careful consideration of alternatives.
_____ I feel that it is better if people always engage in a careful consideration of alternatives.

13. **Social Aspects of College Life** (check one)

_____ In general, I am very much against an emphasis on the social aspects of college life.
_____ In general, I am against an emphasis on the social aspects of college life.
_____ In general, I am mildly against an emphasis on the social aspects of college life.
_____ In general, I am mildly in favor of an emphasis on the social aspects of college life.
_____ In general, I am in favor of an emphasis on the social aspects of college life.
_____ In general, I am very much in favor of an emphasis on the social aspects of college life.

14. **Birth Control** (check one)

_____ I am very much in favor of most birth control techniques.
_____ I am in favor of most birth control techniques.
_____ I am mildly in favor of most birth control techniques.
_____ I am mildly opposed to most birth control techniques.
_____ I am opposed to most birth control techniques.
_____ I am very much opposed to most birth control techniques.

15. **Classical Music** (check one)

_____ I dislike classical music very much.
_____ I dislike classical music.
_____ I dislike classical music to a slight degree.
_____ I enjoy classical music to a slight degree.
_____ I enjoy classical music.
_____ I enjoy classical music very much.

16. **Drinking** (check one)

_____ In general, I am very much in favor of college students drinking alcoholic beverages.
_____ In general, I am in favor of college students drinking alcoholic beverages.
_____ In general, I am mildly in favor of college students drinking alcoholic beverages.
_____ In general, I am mildly opposed to college students drinking alcoholic beverages.
_____ In general, I am opposed to college students drinking alcoholic beverages.
_____ In general, I am very much opposed to college students drinking alcoholic beverages.

17. American Way of Life (check one)

_____ I strongly believe that the American way of life is not the best.
_____ I believe that the American way of life is not the best.
_____ I feel that perhaps the American way of life is not the best.
_____ I feel that perhaps the American way of life is the best.
_____ I believe that the American way of life is the best.
_____ I strongly believe that the American way of life is the best.

18. Sports (check one)

_____ I enjoy sports very much.
_____ I enjoy sports.
_____ I enjoy sports to a slight degree.
_____ I dislike sports to a slight degree.
_____ I dislike sports.
_____ I dislike sports very much.

19. Premarital Sex Relations (check one)

_____ In general, I am very much opposed to premarital sex relations.
_____ In general, I am opposed to premarital sex relations.
_____ In general, I am mildly opposed to premarital sex relations.
_____ In general, I am mildly in favor of premarital sex relations.
_____ In general, I am in favor of premarital sex relations.
_____ In general, I am very much in favor of premarital sex relations.

20. Science Fiction (check one)

_____ I enjoy science fiction very much.
_____ I enjoy science fiction.
_____ I enjoy science fiction to a slight degree.
_____ I dislike science fiction to a slight degree.
_____ I dislike science fiction.
_____ I dislike science fiction very much.

21. Money (check one)

_____ I strongly believe that money is not one of the most important goals in life.
_____ I believe that money is not one of the most important goals in life.
_____ I feel that perhaps money is not one of the most important goals in life.
_____ I feel that perhaps moneys is one of the most important goals in life.
_____ I believe that money is one of the most important goals in life.
_____ I strongly believe that money is one of the most important goals in life.

22. Grades (check one)

_____ I am very much in favor of the university grading system as it now exists.
_____ I am in favor of the university grading system as it now exists.
_____ I am slightly in favor of the university grading system as it now exists.
_____ I am slightly opposed to the university grading system as it now exists.
_____ I am opposed to the university grading system as it now exists.
_____ I am very much opposed to the university grading system as it now exists.

23. Political Parties (check one)

_____ I am a strong supporter of the Democratic party.
_____ I prefer the Democratic party.
_____ I have a slight preference to the Democratic party.
_____ I have a slight preference to the Republican party.
_____ I prefer the Republican party.
_____ I am a strong supporter of the Republican party.

24. Group Opinion (check one)

_____ I feel that people should always ignore group opinion if they disagree with it.
_____ I feel that people should usually ignore group opinion if they disagree with it.
_____ I feel that people should often ignore group opinion if they disagree with it.
_____ I feel that people should often go along with group opinion even if they disagree with it.
_____ I feel that people should usually go along with group opinion even if they disagree with it.
_____ I feel that people should always go along with group opinion even if they disagree with it.

25. One True Religion (check one)

_____ I strongly believe that my church represents the one true religion.
_____ I believe that my church represents the one true religion.
_____ I feel that probably my church represents the one true religion.
_____ I feel that probably no church represents the one true religion.
_____ I believe that no church represents the one true religion.
_____ I strongly believe that no church represents the one true religion.

26. Musical Comedies (check one)

_____ I dislike musical comedies very much.
_____ I dislike musical comedies.
_____ I dislike musical comedies to a slight degree.
_____ I enjoy musical comedies to a slight degree.
_____ I enjoy musical comedies.
_____ I enjoy musical comedies very much.

27. Preparedness for War (check one)

_____ I strongly believe that preparedness for war will not tend to precipitate war.
_____ I believe that preparedness for war will not tend to precipitate war.
_____ I feel that perhaps preparedness for war will not tend to precipitate war.
_____ I feel that perhaps preparedness for war will tend to precipitate war.
_____ I believe that preparedness for war will tend to precipitate war.
_____ I strongly believe that preparedness for war will tend to precipitate war.

28. Welfare Legislation (check one)

_____ I am very much opposed to increased welfare legislation.
_____ I am opposed to increased welfare legislation.
_____ I am mildly opposed to increased welfare legislation.
_____ I am mildly in favor of increased welfare legislation.
_____ I am in favor of increased welfare legislation.
_____ I am very much in favor of increased welfare legislation.

29. Creative Work (check one)

_____ I enjoy doing creative work very much.
_____ I enjoy doing creative work.
_____ I enjoy doing creative work to a slight degree.
_____ I dislike doing creative work to a slight degree.
_____ I dislike doing creative work.
_____ I dislike doing creative work very much.

30. Dating (check one)

_____ I strongly believe that girls should be allowed to date before they are in high school.
_____ I believe that girls should be allowed to date before they are in high school.
_____ I feel that perhaps girls should be allowed to date before they are in high school.
_____ I feel that perhaps girls should not be allowed to date before they are in high school.
_____ I believe that girls should not be allowed to date before they are in high school.
_____ I strongly believe that girls should not be allowed to date before they are in high school.

31. Red China and the U.N.[3] (check one)

_____ I strongly believe that Red China should not be admitted to the U.N.
_____ I believe that Red China should not be admitted to the U.N.
_____ I feel that perhaps Red China should not be admitted to the U.N.
_____ I feel that perhaps Red China should be admitted to the U.N.
_____ I believe that Red China should be admitted to the U.N.
_____ I strongly believe that Red China should be admitted to the U.N.

32. Novels (check one)

_____ I dislike reading novels very much.
_____ I dislike reading novels.
_____ I dislike reading novels to a slight degree.
_____ I enjoy reading novels to a slight degree.
_____ I enjoy reading novels.
_____ I enjoy reading novels very much.

33. Socialized Medicine (check one)

_____ I am very much opposed to socialized medicine as it operates in Great Britain.
_____ I am opposed to socialized medicine as it operates in Great Britain.
_____ I am mildly opposed to socialized medicine as it operates in Great Britain.
_____ I am mildly in favor of socialized medicine as it operates in Great Britain.
_____ I am in favor of socialized medicine as it operates in Great Britain.
_____ I am very much in favor of socialized medicine as it operates in Great Britain.

34. War (check one)

_____ I strongly feel that war is sometimes necessary to solve world problems.
_____ I feel that war is sometimes necessary to solve world problems.
_____ I feel that perhaps war is sometimes necessary to solve world problems.
_____ I feel that perhaps war is never necessary to solve world problems.
_____ I feel that war is never necessary to solve world problems.
_____ I strongly feel that war is never necessary to solve world problems.

Authors note: To update this question, you may wish to change "Red China" to "People's Republic of China" and use a more current issue, such as that of the United States' diplomatic relations with China.

35. **State Income Tax** (check one)

_____ I am very much opposed to a state income tax.
_____ I am opposed to a state income tax.
_____ I am mildly opposed to a state income tax.
_____ I am mildly in favor of a state income tax.
_____ I am in favor of a state income tax.
_____ I am very much in favor to a state income tax.

36. **Tipping** (check one)

_____ I am very much opposed to the custom of tipping.
_____ I am opposed to the custom of tipping.
_____ I am mildly opposed to the custom of tipping.
_____ I am mildly in favor of the custom of tipping.
_____ I am in favor of the custom of tipping.
_____ I am very much in favor of the custom of tipping.

37. **Pets** (check one)

_____ I enjoy keeping pets very much.
_____ I enjoy keeping pets.
_____ I enjoy keeping pets to a slight degree.
_____ I dislike keeping pets to a slight degree.
_____ I dislike keeping pets.
_____ I dislike keeping pets very much.

38. **Foreign Movies** (check one)

_____ I enjoy foreign movies very much.
_____ I enjoy foreign movies.
_____ I enjoy foreign movies to a slight degree.
_____ I dislike foreign movies to a slight degree.
_____ I dislike foreign movies.
_____ I dislike foreign movies very much.

39. **Strict Discipline** (check one)

_____ I am very much against strict disciplining of children.
_____ I am against strict disciplining of children.
_____ I am mildly against strict disciplining of children.
_____ I am mildly in favor of strict disciplining of children.
_____ I am in favor of strict disciplining of children.
_____ I am very much in favor of strict disciplining of children.

40. **Financial Help From Parents** (check one)

_____ I strongly believe that parents should provide financial help to young married couples.
_____ I believe that parents should provide financial help to young married couples.
_____ I feel that perhaps parents should provide financial help to young married couples.
_____ I feel that perhaps parents should not provide financial help to young married couples.
_____ I believe that parents should not provide financial help to young married couples.
_____ I strongly believe that parents should not provide financial help to young married couples.

41. **Freshman Having Cars on Campus (check one)**

_____ I am very much in favor of freshmen being allowed to have cars on campus.
_____ I am in favor of freshmen being allowed to have cars on campus.
_____ I am in favor of freshmen being allowed to have cars on campus to a slight degree.
_____ I am against freshmen being allowed to have cars on campus to a slight degree.
_____ I am against freshmen being allowed to have cars on campus.
_____ I am very much against freshmen being allowed to have cars on campus.

42. **Foreign Language (check one)**

_____ I am very much in favor of requiring students to learn a foreign language.
_____ I am in favor of requiring students to learn a foreign language.
_____ I am mildly in favor of requiring students to learn a foreign language.
_____ I am mildly opposed to requiring students to learn a foreign language.
_____ I am opposed to requiring students to learn a foreign language.
_____ I am very much opposed to requiring students to learn a foreign language.

43. **College Education (check one)**

_____ I strongly believe it is very important for a person to have a college education in order to be successful.
_____ I believe it is very important for a person to have a college education in order to be successful.
_____ I believe that perhaps it is very important for a person to have a college education in order to be successful.
_____ I believe that perhaps it is not very important for a person to have a college education in order to be successful.
_____ I believe that it is not very important for a person to have a college education in order to be successful.
_____ I strongly believe that it is not very important for a person to have a college education in order to be successful.

44. **Fresh Air and Exercise (check one)**

_____ I strongly believe that fresh air and daily exercise are not important.
_____ I believe that fresh air and daily exercise are not important.
_____ I feel that probably fresh air and daily exercise are not important.
_____ I feel that probably fresh air and daily exercise are important.
_____ I believe fresh air and daily exercise are important.
_____ I strongly believe that fresh air and daily exercise are important.

45. **Discipline of Children (check one)**

_____ I strongly believe that the father should discipline the children in the family.
_____ I believe that the father should discipline the children in the family.
_____ I feel that perhaps the father should discipline the children in the family.
_____ I feel that perhaps the mother should discipline the children in the family.
_____ I believe that the mother should discipline the children in the family.
_____ I strongly believe that the mother should discipline the children in the family.

46. **Nuclear Arms Race (check one)**

_____ I am very much opposed to the federal government's buildup of nuclear arms.
_____ I am opposed to the federal government's buildup of nuclear arms.
_____ I am mildly opposed to the federal government's buildup of nuclear arms.
_____ I am mildly in favor of the federal government's buildup of nuclear arms.
_____ I am in favor of the federal government's buildup of nuclear arms.
_____ I am very much in favor of the federal government's buildup of nuclear arms.

47. **Community Bomb Shelters** (check one)

____ I strongly believe that the federal government should provide community bomb shelters.
____ I believe that the federal government should provide community bomb shelters.
____ I feel that perhaps the federal government should provide community bomb shelters.
____ I feel that perhaps individuals should provide their own bomb shelters.
____ I believe that individuals should provide their own bomb shelters.
____ I strongly believe that individuals should provide their own bomb shelters.

48. **Divorce** (check one)

____ I am very much opposed to divorce.
____ I am opposed to divorce.
____ I am mildly opposed to divorce.
____ I am mildly in favor of divorce.
____ I am in favor of divorce.
____ I am very much in favor of divorce.

49. **Gardening** (check one)

____ I enjoy gardening very much.
____ I enjoy gardening.
____ I enjoy gardening to a slight degree.
____ I dislike gardening to a slight degree.
____ I dislike gardening.
____ I dislike gardening very much.

50. **Dancing** (check one)

____ I enjoy dancing very much.
____ I enjoy dancing.
____ I enjoy dancing to a slight degree.
____ I dislike dancing to a slight degree.
____ I dislike dancing.
____ I dislike dancing very much.

51. **A Catholic President** (check one)

____ I am very much in favor of a Catholic being elected president.
____ I am in favor of a Catholic being elected president.
____ I am mildly in favor of a Catholic being elected president.
____ I am mildly against a Catholic being elected president.
____ I am against a Catholic being elected president.
____ I am very much against a Catholic being elected president.

52. **Women in Today's Society** (check one)

____ I strongly believe that women are not taking too aggressive a role in society today.
____ I believe that women are not taking too aggressive a role in society today.
____ I feel that perhaps women are not taking too aggressive a role in society today.
____ I feel that perhaps women are taking too aggressive a role in society today.
____ I believe that women are taking too aggressive a role in society today.
____ I strongly believe that women are taking too aggressive a role in society today.

53. Family Finances (check one)

_____ I strongly believe that the man in the family should handle the finances.
_____ I believe that the man in the family should handle the finances.
_____ I feel that perhaps the man in the family should handle the finances.
_____ I feel that perhaps the woman in the family should handle the finances.
_____ I believe that the woman in the family should handle the finances.
_____ I strongly believe that the woman in the family should handle the finances.

54. Exhibitions of Modern Art (check one)

_____ I dislike looking at exhibitions of modern art very much.
_____ I dislike looking at exhibitions of modern art.
_____ I dislike looking at exhibitions of modern art to a slight degree.
_____ I enjoy looking at exhibitions of modern art to a slight degree.
_____ I enjoy looking at exhibitions of modern art.
_____ I enjoy looking at exhibitions of modern art very much.

55. Careers for Women (check one)

_____ I am very much in favor of women pursuing careers.
_____ I am in favor of women pursuing careers.
_____ I am mildly in favor of women pursuing careers.
_____ I am mildly opposed to women pursuing careers.
_____ I am opposed to women pursuing careers.
_____ I am very much opposed to women pursuing careers.

56. Men's Adjustment to Stress (check one)

_____ I strongly believe that men adjust to stress better than women.
_____ I believe that men adjust to stress better than women.
_____ I feel that perhaps men adjust to stress better than women.
_____ I feel that perhaps men do not adjust to stress better than women.
_____ I believe that men do not adjust to stress better than women.
_____ I strongly believe that men do not adjust to stress better than women.

INTERPERSONAL JUDGEMENT SCALE

1. Intelligence (check one)

_____ I believe that this person is very much above average in intelligence.
_____ I believe that this person is above average in intelligence.
_____ I believe that this person is slightly above average in intelligence.
_____ I believe that this person is average in intelligence.
_____ I believe that this person is slightly below average in intelligence.
_____ I believe that this person is below average in intelligence.
_____ I believe that this person is very much below average in intelligence.

2. Knowledge of Current Events (check one)

_____ I believe that this person is very much below average in his(her) knowledge of current events.
_____ I believe that this person is below average in his(her) knowledge of current events.
_____ I believe that this person is slightly below average in his(her) knowledge of current events.
_____ I believe that this person is average in his(her) knowledge of current events.
_____ I believe that this person is slightly above average in his(her) knowledge of current events.
_____ I believe that this person is above average in his(her) knowledge of current events.
_____ I believe that this person is very much above average in his(her) knowledge of current events.

3. Morality (check one)

_____ This person impresses me as being extremely moral.
_____ This person impresses me as being moral.
_____ This person impresses me as being moral to a slight degree.
_____ This person impresses me as being neither moral nor particularly immoral.
_____ This person impresses me as being immoral to a slight degree.
_____ This person impresses me as being immoral.
_____ This person impresses me as being extremely immoral.

4. Adjustment (check one)

_____ I believe that this person is extremely maladjusted.
_____ I believe that this person is maladjusted.
_____ I believe that this person is maladjusted to a slight degree.
_____ I believe that this person is neither particularly maladjusted nor particularly well adjusted.
_____ I believe that this person is well adjusted to a slight degree.
_____ I believe that this person is well adjusted.
_____ I believe that this person is extremely well adjusted.

5. Personal Feelings (check one)

_____ I feel that I would probably like this person very much.
_____ I feel that I would probably like this person.
_____ I feel that I would probably like this person to a slight degree.
_____ I feel that I would probably neither particularly like nor particularly dislike this person.
_____ I feel that I would probably dislike this person to a slight degree.
_____ I feel that I would probably dislike this person.
_____ I feel that I would probably dislike this person very much.

6. Working Together in an Experiment (check one)

_____ I believe that I would very much dislike working with this person in an experiment.
_____ I believe that I would dislike working with this person in an experiment.
_____ I believe that I would dislike working with this person in an experiment to a slight degree.
_____ I believe that I would neither particularly dislike nor particularly like working with this person in an experiment.
_____ I believe that I would enjoy working with this person in an experiment to a slight degree.
_____ I believe that I would enjoy working with this person in an experiment.
_____ I believe that I would very much enjoy working with this person in an experiment.

TOPIC 12:   QUASI-EXPERIMENTAL DESIGNS

Topic 12 is also concerned with the design of experiments. Here the goal is to provide you with experience in designing quasi-experimental studies that must be conducted within the natural setting of the real world.

In quasi-experimental research the investigator does not have the degree of control over antecedent conditions or extraneous variables that he or she may have within the confines of the laboratory. Whenever we move outside the laboratory we still typically have control over the presentation of the independent variable. However, we frequently loose the ability to randomly assign participants to experimental treatment conditions. As a result, our participants are probably not equated at the outset of the experiment and thus a quasi-experiment is the only type of experiment that can be conducted. As far as possible the experimenter should attempt to control for extraneous variables. Since the natural environment has many more extraneous variables potentially affecting the independent variables, the experimenter must always be prepared to evaluate any such variables noted during the course of the experiment. The quasi-experimental design must be constructed in such a manner as to rule out any rival hypothesis whose effect cannot be controlled.

For each of the laboratory exercises in this Topic, you will be given background material on a specific problem area. Your task is to read the introductory material and the statement of the problem and then to design an experiment which would provide an answer to the research problem being asked. Each of these quasi-experiments are to be designed so that they are carried out in a natural setting. Your instructor will assign all or some of the following laboratory exercises.

LABORATORY EXERCISE 1: THE EFFECTS OF ROLE CHANGE ON ATTITUDES

Each individual, engaging in everyday activities, is required to assume at different times a variety of different roles, including spouse, parent, employer or employee, and friend. Each role has an accompanying set of expected behaviors. Role theory makes the assumption that a person's attitudes will be influenced by the role which he or she occupies. If a person made a change in roles from being a renter to a home-owner, there might be a corresponding change in attitude toward care of the home. This change should be one that is congruent with being a home owner.

Although this assumption of role theory is quite logical, there has been little experimental support for its existence. Some correlational evidence does, however, exist. For example, it has been found that commissioned officers are more favorably disposed toward the army than are enlisted men. The problem with such evidence is that it is correlational, and therefore, does not rule out the possibility that the men who are initially proarmy are the ones who become commissioned, rather than being commissioned leading to positive attitudes. Consequently, there is no clear-cut evidence of the causal relationships. In order to obtain such evidence it would be necessary to conduct a longitudinal study where role changes naturally occurred for some individuals. One such setting would be that of an industrial organization that promoted individuals to the level of supervisor from within the ranks of their employees.

Assume that you had identified a company that met such a standard and would allow you to conduct a study which would test this proposition of role theory. Assume also that the company was unionized and that there were approximately as many workers who served as supervisors as served as stewards in the union (about 150 of each). From role theory one would predict that the workers who became stewards would develop more prounion attitudes and the workers who became supervisors would develop a more procompany attitude.

Your task is to design an experiment that would test these predictions which were derived from role theory. On a separate sheet of paper, write the method section following the APA Publication guidelines. A method section includes the subsections of participants; apparatus, instruments, or other materials; and procedure. Turn in the completed method section to your instructor.

Roles References:

Pina, D. L., & Bengtson, V. L. (1993). The division of household labor and wives' happiness: Ideology, employment and perceptions of support. *Journal of Marriage and the Family, 55*, 901-912.

Johnson, W. R., Johnson, G. J., & Patterson, C. R. (1999). Moderators of the relationship between company and union commitment: A meta-analysis. *Journal of Psychology, 133*, 85-103.

LABORATORY EXERCISE 2: EMPLOYEE PARTICIPATION IN INCENTIVE PAY PLAN

In the past, many incentive pay plans have been imposed by a variety of companies in an attempt to accomplish the goals of increased productivity and sales, and reduced cost, absenteeism, and turnover. Prior research that has investigated the relative impact of such attempts has produced extremely conflicting results. One study would demonstrate the effectiveness of a given incentive pay plan whereas another study would yield results demonstrating its ineffectiveness. Such conflicting results suggest that other factors are having a moderating effect on the pay incentive plan, and research needs to be conducted to isolate the variables that make a given plan effective for one company but not for another company. One such moderating factor could be the way in which a given pay plan is developed and introduced to the employees. Pay incentive plans could, for example, be developed by the management and imposed upon the employer. On the other hand, pay incentive plans could be developed by the employees and subjected to approval by management. If the employees develop the pay plan they are more likely to be committed to its success as well as having greater understanding of it. Additionally, it is more likely to be appropriate to the employees' working situation. Therefore, the present study will investigate the relative effectiveness of pay plans developed by employees as opposed to those developed by management. It is hypothesized that the most effective pay plan will be the one that the employees develop.

Your task is to design an experiment that would investigate this hypothesis.

On a separate sheet of paper, write the method section following the APA Publication Manual guidelines. A method section includes the subsections of participants; apparatus, instruments, or other materials; and procedure. Turn in the completed method section to your instructor.

Pay Plan References:

Rowland, D. C., & Greene, B. (1987). Incentive pay: Productivity's own reward. *Personnel Journal, 66*, 48-57.

Stein, A. D., Karel, T., & Zuidema, R. (1999). Carrots and sticks: impact of an incentive/disincentive employee flexible credit benefit plan on health status and medical costs. *American Journal of Health Promotion, 13*, 260-267.

LABORATORY EXERCISE 3: INTELLIGENCE AND ACHIEVEMENT -- WHICH IS THE CAUSAL AGENT?

In looking at the literature on cognitive development one finds two opposing models of mental growth. On the one hand, there is the model that purports that intelligence causes achievement. Such a model was advocated by men such as Francis Galton, Charles Darwin, and Cyril Burt, and supported by the results of numerous studies of twins reared separately. These studies have consistently revealed that the correlation of the intelligence of identical twins reared separately is consistently greater than that of siblings reared apart and also greater than that found between unrelated persons. If the causal relationship was from achievement to intelligence then the intelligence test scores of these twins should not exceed chance and definitely not exceed that of unrelated persons or siblings reared apart.

The other model holds that the causal relationship is from achievement to intelligence. Such a model would be emphasized by such individuals as Piaget. Although Piaget recognized the basic importance of inborn processes, he relegated them to a secondary position in the determination of intelligence and achievement. Of primary importance was the acquisition of skills, rules, and information, which when combined resulted in the formation of higher order and more abstract and generalized principles or, in other words, resulted in greater intelligence.

This controversy of the causal order of the intelligence-achievement sequence reveals that the issue has yet to be solved. The basic issue to be solved here is identification of the preponderant causal relationship. It is highly unlikely that one of the two models of mental growth is totally inaccurate and the other totally accurate. Rather, a more probable picture is that intelligence and achievement are both causally related in a feedback loop system. However, one of these two is undoubtedly the more important causal agent.

Your task is to design a study that will investigate the causal relationship between intelligence and achievement to determine which factor is the preponderant causal agent.

On a separate paper of paper, write the method section following the APA Publication Manual guideline. A method section includes the subsections of participants; apparatus, instruments, or other materials; and procedure. Turn in the completed method section to your instructor.

Intelligence References:

Cotte, J. E., & Levine, C. G. (2000). Attitude versus aptitude: Is intelligence or motivation more important for positive higher-educational outcomes? *Journal of Adolescent Research 15*, 58-80.

Irvine, S. H., & Berry, J. W.(Eds.) (1988). *Human abilities in cultural context*. New York: Cambridge University Press.

Gardner, H., Kornhaber, M. L., & Wake, W. K. (1996). *Intelligence: Multiple perspectives*. Ft Worth, TX: Harcourt Brace College Publishers.

Shafer, A. B. (1999). Relation of the Big Five and Factor V subcomponents to Social Intelligence. *European Journal of Personality, 13*, 225-240.

Snyder, R. F. (2000). The relationship between learning styles/multiple intelligences and academic achievement of high school students. *High School Journal, 83*, 11-20.

LABORATORY EXERCISE 4: JAY WALKING BEHAVIOR

Assume that you had observed that some people violate traffic signals and cross the street in spite of the fact that the traffic signal is flashing "wait". You want to know what factors motivate individuals to violate such prohibitions. However, in designing such a study it would be very difficult to randomly assign participants to appear at various street crossings at different times during the day to correspond with your experimental treatment conditions. Therefore, the design in most instances must be of the quasi-experimental variety.

Lefkowitz, Blake, and Mouton (1955) used such a design several decades ago. They postulated that one of the variables motivating jaywalking behavior was the presence of a model. In other words, if another person jaywalked first you may be also more prone to jaywalk. They found, in investigating this phenomenon, that the presence of such a model is effective only when the model is a high status model. Mullen, Copper and Driskell (1990) reviewed seven studies that examined the effects of model behavior on pedestrian jaywalking.

What other factors might influence a person's decision to jaywalk? Your task is to identify at least three possible variables which you hypothesize have an influence upon jaywalking. Then design an experiment which would allow you to test experimentally the influence of these variables. In designing the experiment you must decide on a number of factors, such as the following: (1) At what point has a person jaywalked? Is it when they have completely crossed the street? What if the person only crossed the street part of the way and then turned around and returned to the curb? (2) What individuals will you include as potential participants for the experiment? People may be continuously approaching the curb. Be attentive to possible confounds.

Listed below is some background reading if you wish to pursue this topic more thoroughly. This experiment could be carried out if you informed the local police department of your intent and obtained their permission, as well as the permission of your human participants' committee.

Jaywalking References:

Jason, L. A., & Liotta, R. F. (1982). Pedestrian jaywalking under facilitating and nonfacilitating conditions. *Journal of Applied Behavior Analysis, 15,* 469-473.

Jorgensen, N. D. (1988). Risky behavior at traffic signals: A traffic engineer's view. Special issue: Risky decision-making in transport operations. *Ergonomics, 31,* 657-661.

Lefkowitz, M., Blake, R. R., & Mouton, J. S. (1955). Status factors in pedestrian violation of traffic signals. *Journal of Abnormal and Social Psychology, 51,* 704-706.

Mullen, B., Copper, C., & Driskell, J. E. (1990). Jaywalking as a function of model behavior. *Personality and Social Psychology Bulletin, 16,* 320-330.

Russell, J. C., Wilson, D. O., & Jenkins, J. F. (1976). Informational properties of jaywalking: An extension to model sex, race and number. *Sociometry, 39,* 270-273.

Segelman, C. K., & Segelman, L. (1976). Authority and conformity: Violation of a traffic regulation. *The Journal of Social Psychology, 100,* 35-43.

van Houton, R. (1988). The effects of advance stop lines and sign prompts on pedestrian safety in a crosswalk on a multilane highway. *Journal of Applied Behavior Analysis, 21,* 245-251.

TOPIC 13: SINGLE-CASE AND SINGLE-GROUP DESIGNS

The laboratory goals of Topic 13 are to provide you with experience in identifying and designing single-case and single-group designs.

As noted in the preface to *Methodological and conceptual issues in applied behavior analysis: 1968-1988* (Iwata, 1989),

> Originally developed in operant conditioning laboratories, the single-subject [single-case] approach represents a clear departure from research methods typical of most other areas of psychology and the social sciences, by placing greater emphasis on the objective measurement of ongoing behavior, the collection of extended data samples per individual subject, the use of a subject's behavioral "baseline" as a control condition for the purpose of conducting experimental comparisons, and the evaluation of experimental effects through visual examination of data (p.iii).

Single-case and single-group studies use some form of a time-series design. Repeated measurements are taken on the dependent variable both before and after a treatment condition is introduced. The most basic design is an <u>A-B-A design</u> with three conditions: A - the baseline; B - the experimental treatment; and, A - the second baseline that is reintroduced without the treatment. For further information about this basic A-B-A design, refer to your textbook for discussion and examples.

Another approach is the <u>multiple-baseline design</u>. Often in an A-B-A design the second baseline condition does not return to the original baseline. This creates ambiguous results so that one cannot completely eliminate a rival hypothesis. To overcome this deficit, some researchers use a multiple baseline design and examine the same person (or group) over several situations, different people (groups) over the same situations, or several behaviors for the same individual. This design might involve taking a baseline measure on two participants and then administering the treatment condition to one of the participants while the other remained in the baseline condition. Only after the treatment condition had been administered to the first participant would it be administered to the second participant.

More elaborate designs are also found in the literature. <u>Interaction designs</u> permit the experimenters to evaluate different levels of the independent variables (treatment) in comparison to the baseline condition. For instance, a researcher might examine the effect of verbal reinforcement ("very good") and food reinforcement (candy) on eye contact with autistic children. The variables could be examined alone and with one another, in comparison to the baseline phase(s).

Finally, another design is the <u>changing-criterion design</u>. The target behavior is examined first in a baseline condition. Then a treatment is applied until a certain criterion is obtained. Once the initial criterion of successful performance is met, the experimenter changes the criterion level until the altered criterion is met. For instance, a disruptive child in the classroom might be given a reward (playing games on a computer) if he or she sits still 15% of the time. Once that criterion is met, the teacher may change the criterion to 25% of the time, and so on.

Reference:

Iwata, B. A. (Ed.) (1989). *Methodological and conceptual issues in applied behavior analysis: 1968-1988.* US: Society for the Experimental Analysis of Behavior.

LABORATORY EXERCISE 1: EVALUATING SINGLE-CASE DESIGNS IN PUBLISHED RESEARCH

The purpose of this laboratory exercise is to give you experience in identifying and analyzing single-case designs.

Your assignment for this laboratory exercise is to go to the library and find a single-case design experiment. Excellent journals which often report such studies are *Behavior Therapy, Experimental Analysis of Behavior*, and *Journal of Applied Behavior Analysis*. The *Journal of Applied Behavior Analysis* has study questions at the end of each article, something we have not found in other journals. Your instructor may ask you to answer these questions as well.

Answer the following on a separate sheet of paper and hand into your instructor.

1. Give the complete reference of the study.

2. What was the purpose of the study?

3. What were the hypotheses?

4. Describe the method in detail.

    a. Who was (were) the participant(s)? How was the participant chosen?

    b. Identify which kind of design was used. Describe it in detail.

    c. Identify the independent variable(s). If it changes in any manner during the course of the experiment, explain how it did.

    d. Identify the dependent variable(s).

5. Describe the major results.

6. Describe the conclusions of the author(s). Are they warranted?

7. Are there any rival interpretations of the results? If so, discuss them briefly.

LABORATORY EXERCISE 2: DESIGNING SINGLE-GROUP STUDY -- INCREASING SAFETY SEAT BELT USAGE

The purpose of this laboratory exercise is to give you experience in evaluating a single-group study and in designing a subsequent study.

Behavior change interventions are used not only in clinical settings but also in public domains by community and applied experimental psychologists. Examples of such intervention research programs include increasing the collection of recyclables (e.g., Geller, Winett, & Everett, 1982), increasing conservation behaviors (e.g., Geller et al., 1982), increasing safety belt usage (e.g., Geller, 1988), reducing AIDS risk behaviors (Kelly, St. Lawrence, Hood, & Brasfield, 1990), and other health behaviors (Elder, Geller, Hovell, & Mayer, 1994).

A major public health problem is automobile crash-induced injuries, many of which could be reduced in severity if automobile occupants had used safety belts. Legislature has been enacted in numerous states, using negative reinforcement and punishment (punative fines), to insure that automobile occupants use safety belts and still people often do not follow the law. As Thyer and Geller (1987) note, "Such belt use mandates are usually only moderately effective, unless they are rigorously enforced (see Jonah et al., 1982), and they have the disadvantage of imposing additional elements of aversive control on citizens already burdened with a surfeit of punitive legal sanctions" (p. 485). Rather, they advocate the use of positive reinforcement contingencies to get the general public to comply with buckling up.

Psychologists have used a number of techniques to motivate safety belt usage with mixed success (e.g., Boyce & Geller, 1999; Grossman & Garcia, 1999; Streff & Geller, 1986). Geller (1988) refers to an "ABC" model for behavior change: activator -- behavior -- consequence. Activators (reminder, prompt, model education, commitment, incentive, disincentive) produce a behavior (safety belt use) which in turn results in a consequence (reward or positive reinforcer, punisher or negative reinforcer). The use of a vehicle dashboard sticker (a prompt) that read "SAFETY BELT USE REQUIRED IN THIS VEHICLE" substantially increased safety belt use in a study by Thyer and Geller (1987). They used an A (baseline) - B (intervention of stickers) - A (withdrawal of stickers) - B (intervention of stickers) design. Safety belt use ranged from 17% to 50% (Mean = 34%) of the passengers in the first baseline. By the end of the second intervention phase, safety belt use ranged from 54% to 90% (Mean = 78%) of the front-seat passengers. The figure[1] at the end of this section shows the percentage of vehicle passengers who bucked up in the different conditions.

On the following pages is reprinted the complete article by Thyer, Geller, Williams, and Purcell (1987) in which they used an A-B-A-B design to study the effectiveness of a community-based prompting intervention on a university campus. You are to read critically this article and then design a similar single-group A-B-A-B study that would be feasible to carry out on your campus or in your community. Pay close attention to the design of the prompts and how you will make them visible to drivers. Consider issues for future research that Thyer et al. present in their discussion section, and determine how you can address them in your study. Write up the method section for this proposed study.

---

[1]From Thyer and Geller (1987, p. 490). Copyright 1987 by Sage Publication, Inc. Reprinted by permission.

We hope that you will actually carry out the study in such a manner that it is publishable in a psychological journal. From research laboratory courses such as the one you are presently in come many projects that can be carried out in future semesters as independent research projects. Large and colorful "Flash-for-Life" cards are available from E. Scott Geller (Department of Psychology, Virginia Polytechnic Institute and State University, Blacksburg, VA 24061) for a nominal cost.

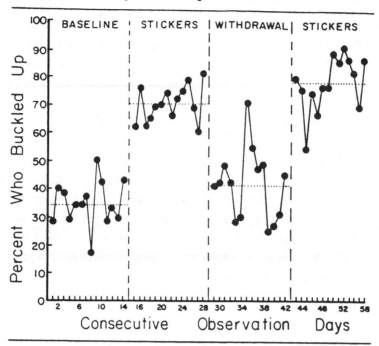

The percentage of passengers who buckled up over 58 consecutive observation days, two-weeks per consecutive baseline, intervention, withdrawal, and intervention phase.

References:

Boyce, T. E., & Geller, E. S. (1999). Attempts to increase vehicle safety-belt use among industry workers: What can we learn from our failures? *Journal of Organizational Behavior Management, 19*, 27-44.

Elder, J. P., Geller, E.S., Hovell, M.F., & Mayer, J.A. (1994). *Motivating health behavior*. Albany, NY: Delmar Publishers Inc.

Geller, E.S. (1988). A behavioral science approach to transportation safety. *Bulletin of the New York Academy of Medicine, 64*, 632-661.

Geller, E.S., Winett, R.A., & Everett, P.B. (1982). *Preserving the environment: New strategies for behavior change*. New York: Pergamon.

Grossman, D. C., & Garcia, C. C. (1999). Effectiveness of health promotion programs to increase motor vehicle occupant restraint use among young children. *American Journal of Preventive Medicine, 16*, 12-22.

Johan, B.A., Dawson, N.E., & Smith, G.A. (1982). Effects of a selective traffic enforcement program on seat belt use. *Journal of Applied Psychology, 67*, 84-96.

Kelly, J. A., St. Lawrence, J. S., Hood, H. V., & Brasfield, T. L. (1990). Behavioral intervention to reduce AIDS risk activities. *Journal of Consulting and Clinical Psychology, 57*, 60-67.

Ludwig, T. D., & Geller, E. S. (1999). Behavior change among agents of a community safety program: Pizza deliverers advocate community safety belt use. *Journal of Organizational Behavior Management, 19*, 3-24.

Streff, F.M., & Geller, E.S. (1986). Strategies for motivating safety belt use: The application of applied behavior analysis. *Health Education Research: Theory and Practice, 1*, 47-59.

Thyer, B.A., & Geller, E.S. (1987). The "buckle-up" dashboard sticker: An effective environmental intervention for safety belt promotion. *Environment and Behavior, 19*, 484-494.

Thyer, B.A., Geller, E.S., Williams, M., & Purcell, E. (1987). Community-based "flashing" to increase safety belt use. *The Journal of Experimental Education, 55*, 155-159.

Community-Based "Flashing" to Increase Safety Belt Use

BRUCE A. THYER
Florida State University

E. SCOTT GELLER
Virginia Polytechnice Institute
and State University

MELVIN WILLIAMS
ELAINE PURCELL
Florida State University

ABSTRACT

A community-based prompting intervention for safety belt promotion was field tested at two parking lots on a large university campus. The intervention involved a co-ed displaying a flash card that read, "Please buckle up —I care" to unbuckled drivers of vehicles exiting the parking lots. If the driver buckled up, the "flasher" flipped the card over and displayed the message, "Thank you for buckling up." Drivers who were already wearing a shoulder belt when exiting the parking lot were shown only the "thank you" side of the flash card. Simultaneous ABAB paradigms over a 4-week period demonstrated functional control of safety belt use at each parking lot by this prompting intervention. A total of 1,260 flashing episodes occurred and overall compliance with the buckle-up request was 25%. Important issues for follow-up research are discussed, especially the need for further study of the post-intervention, residual effect of prompting that was observed.

EACH YEAR in the United States motor vehicle accidents result in at least 45,000 deaths and 500,000 serious injuries (Bigelow, 1982). In fact, vehicle crashes are the leading cause of fatalities among Americans aged 5 to 34 (Sleet, 1984), and the financial liability of U.S. traffic accidents exceeds $60 billion per year (Pabon, Sims, Smith, & Associates, 1983). It is estimated that 55% of all traffic fatalities and 65% of all injuries would be prevented if vehicle safety belts were used (Department of Transportation, 1983); yet the majority of the Americans do not use this proven safety device.

As a result of the current nationwide efforts to promote safety belt use in the U.S., belt wearing is gradually increasing. Systematic and comprehensive observations of safety belt use by the National Highway Traffic Safety Administration revealed 10.9% belt wearing from 1977 to 1979 (Two Year Study, 1980), and 13.6% safety belt use in 1983 (Steed, 1983). Recently, safety belt use has reached 50% in states that have a safety belt use law (Insurance Institute for Highway Safety, 1985), and has exceeded 60% among employees of corporations that have implemented safety belt incentive programs (e.g., see reviews by Geller, 1984, 1985).

As reviewed recently by Streff and Geller (1986), various strategies have been employed to motivate safety belt use in the U.S., including (a) engineering approaches (e.g., buzzer/light reminders and ignition interlock systems that prevent vehicles from starting unless front seat belts are fastened); (b) legal mandates (from belt use policies at industries and institutions to statewide belt use laws); (c) mass media campaigns (from community billboards to TV and radio spots); (d) education and awareness sessions at industrial sites, schools, civic organizations, and churches; (e) incentive/reward programs at specific corporate, business, and government locations and throughout entire communities; and (f) small-scale reminder strategies (i.e., including highway signs, bumper and dashboard stickers, flyers, and "mailouts").

The present research evaluated the impact of a particular reminder strategy that extended a technique developed recently by Geller and his students, entitled "Flash-for-Life." As described by Geller (1985), a passenger (termed a "flasher") in a stopped vehicle holds a large flash card so that an unbuckled driver or passenger of another stopped vehicle can see the printed message "Please buckle up—I care." If the unbuckled occupant sees the message and buckles up, the flasher flips the card over to reveal the bold message "Thank you for buckling up." In one field study, this simple reminding technique was successful in getting 22% of 893 vehicle occupants who looked at the flash card to buckle up on the spot (Geller, Bruff, & Nimmer, 1985). In the present study, the flash card was not displayed from a vehicle but rather was shown to vehicle occupants as they exited parking lots. This simple modification of the Flash-for-Life technique more effectively reached large numbers of drivers and passengers in a short period of time.

Method

Participants and Setting

The study was conducted on the campus of Florida State University (FSU) during the fall of 1985. Located in Tallahassee, Florida (population 170,000), FSU has approximately 22,000 students and employs 1,700 faculty and staff. At the time of this study the state of Florida did not have a mandatory safety belt use law for adults. Two faculty and staff parking lots adjacent to the school of social work were chosen as intervention sites. The Call Street lot had a capacity of 115 automobiles and could only be entered if the driver had a plastic key-card to open the entrance gate. Key-cards were issued to all faculty and staff who purchased a university parking decal. The Dogwood Way lot had a capacity of 75 automobiles and, although posted signs restricted its use to faculty and staff with parking decals on their automobiles, it could be entered by any driver without such a permit who was willing to risk a $10.00 fine. Both lots were routinely filled to capacity each weekday.

Data Collection

Two graduate students stationed across the street from the single exit of each lot independently recorded whether or not the driver of an exiting vehicle was wearing a shoulder belt. These observations took place Monday through Friday for 4 consecutive weeks from 4:00 P.M. to 5:00 P.M. (the daily peak period of exiting vehicles). Interobserver agreement was calculated using the following formula:

$$A = [\text{agreements}/(\text{agreements} + \text{disagreements})] \times 100$$

The observers were trained to at least an 80% agreement rating prior to collecting data. Each day the

observer-pairs randomly assigned one member to be the primary observer and the other to be the reliability observer.

Intervention

Each parking lot had a permanent stop sign on the passenger's side of exit. As each exiting automobile approached the exit, a female graduate student (i.e., the "flasher"), standing on the driver's side of the parking lot exit, displayed an 11 × 14 inch Flash-for-Life card with the printed message "Please buckle up—I care" to the oncoming driver. The sign was held chest high. If the driver was already wearing a shoulder belt, or was observed buckling up, the flasher reversed the sign to display the message "Thank you for buckling up." Figure 1 illustrates the front and back of the flash card. Flashers did not attempt any other method to prompt or reward safety belt use (e.g., verbal pleas to buckle up or shouts of "thank you").

Design

Baseline. During the first week of data collection, observer-pairs unobtrusively recorded the number of

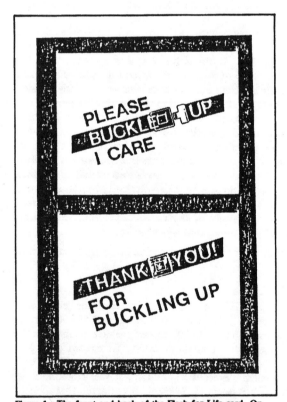

Figure 1—The front and back of the Flash-for-Life card. On both sides the background is white with a 1.3 cm, yellow border; the safety belt is black with yellow letters (3 cm high); the rest of the letters are black (also 3 cm high).

146

vehicles exiting each lot and the number of drivers wearing a shoulder belt. Flashers were not present.

Intervention. During the second week, a flasher displayed a Flash-for-Life card as described previously, and safety belt use was recorded after the vehicle passed the flasher.

The baseline and intervention phases were repeated during the third and fourth weeks, respectively. Thus, the experimental design for each lot represented an ABAB time series (Barlow & Hersen, 1984).

Results

Interobserver Agreement

The number of vehicles exiting daily from the Dogwood Way lot ranged from 49 to 78, with a mean of 63 and totaling 1,250 during 4 weeks. The daily number of exiting vehicles from the Call Street lot ranged from 43 to 78 and also had a mean of 63 exits per day, with a total of 1,268 over 4 weeks. A reliability observer was present for all of the observation periods at the Dogwood Way lot, and for 95% of the observation sessions at the Call Street lot. Daily interobserver reliability ranged from 86% to 100% agreement ($M = 96\%$) at the Dogwood Way lot and from 89% to 100% ($M = 95\%$) at the Call Street lot.

Shoulder Belt Use

Figure 2 shows the daily percentage of shoulder belt use by drivers exiting the two parking lots observed during each of the four experimental conditions. For the Call Street lot, daily shoulder belt use ranged from 19% to 26% ($M = 22\%$) during the first baseline; from 45% to 65% ($M = 52\%$) during the first intervention week; from 34% to 41% ($M = 37\%$) during the second baseline; and from 54% to 68% ($M = 61\%$) during the second intervention.

For vehicles exiting the Dogwood Way lot, driver shoulder belt use ranged from 10% to 21% ($M = 17\%$) during the first baseline; from 32% to 47% ($M = 39\%$) during the first intervention week; from 14% to 25% ($M = 20\%$) during the second baseline week; and from 33% to 52% ($M = 42\%$) during the second intervention phase.

The results demonstrate a relatively powerful effect for the simple prompting intervention. Although the overall number of percentage points increased by the flashing intervention was slightly greater at the Call Street lot than the Dogwood Way lot (i.e., mean increase of 27% vs. 22%, respectively), the overall increase from baseline to intervention was actually higher at the Dogwood Way lot (i.e., 91.5% at Call Street vs. a 119% increase in belt wearing at Dogwood Way). In other words, the prompting procedure almost doubled shoulder belt use by drivers exiting the Call Street lot

and more than doubled the rate of belt use by drivers exiting Dogwood Way.

Functional control of the intervention is clearly shown at both lots by the dramatic decrease in shoulder belt use when prompting was withdrawn (during the second baseline phase) and by the immediate increase in belt wearing at the beginning of the second intervention phase. It is noteworthy, however, that the reversal was not complete, implying that some drivers continued to buckle up after the prompt was removed. The residual effect was markedly higher at the Call Street lot than the Dogwood Way lot. Specifically, at Call Street the second baseline was 15 percentage points higher than the initial baseline (a 68% increase in belt use); whereas at Dogwood Way, the second baseline was only 3 percentage points higher than the initial baseline (a 17.6% increase over baseline).

Social Validity

The flashers reported that occasionally drivers of exiting vehicles paused to offer comments or ask questions. Virtually all such comments were of an approving nature (e.g., thanking the flasher for the reminder to buckle up). Some drivers questioned why the co-ed was engaged in the prompting activity, to which a standard reply was given (i.e., "This is for a class project in the School of Social Work"). Only one driver paused to offer a negative comment, indicating disapproval of safety belts because an acquaintance was trapped inside a flaming vehicle following a collision.

A local television station prepared an on-site news segment about the project, which was aired on three occasions after the study was completed. A local radio station broadcast a similar interview with the senior author, describing the study and the importance of promoting consistent safety belt use.

Discussion

While developing the Flash-for-Life technique, Geller et al. (1985) considered certain characteristics of a verbal or written message that successfully prompted behaviors related to environmental preservation (see review by Geller, Winett, & Everett, 1982). Specifically, the prompt (or message) should be polite, refer to a specific behavior, and occur in close proximity to the requested behavior. Also, the requested behavior should be relatively convenient to emit. In the original Flash-for-Life intervention, Geller et al. (1985) attributed part of their prompting success to the involvement of modeling. That is, the flasher was wearing a readily visible shoulder belt.

The present study showed more pronounced intervention effects than Geller et al. (1985) with an application of the Flash-for-Life technique that did not include modeling and was more cost effective in reaching large

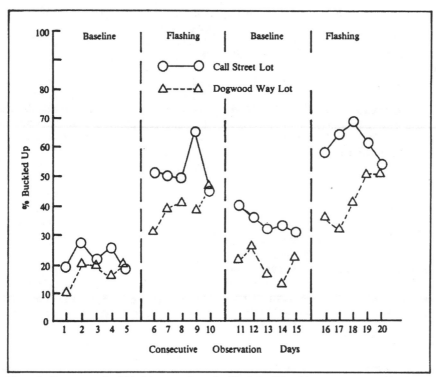

Figure 2—Percentage of vehicle drivers wearing a shoulder belt while exiting two campus parking lots during two baseline periods and two intervention phases when a co-ed displayed a Flash-for-Life card.

numbers of vehicle occupants. In particular, the vehicle-based flashing by Geller et al. took approximately 100 hours to prompt 1,087 unbuckled drivers, and of this total, 17.7% looked at the flash card and complied with the buckle-up request. In the present study, 1,260 drivers were "flashed" in only 20 hours, and although some of these drivers were already buckled up, comparisons with baseline observations indicate that the compliance rates were actually larger than those found by Geller et al. In fact, the overall estimated compliance rate in the present study was 25%. This intervention impact is larger than that found by Geller et al. and is comparable to the outcomes of prior prompting studies that increased the purchase of returnable soft drink containers (Geller, Farris, & Post, 1973) and the appropriate disposal of litter (Geller, Witmer, & Orebaugh, 1976) with specific and polite messages, delivered at the time and place when the requested behavior was convenient to emit.

It is encouraging that shoulder belt use during the second baseline phase was higher than initial baseline levels, especially at the Call Street lot. This suggests that the prompting intervention had more than transient impact on some drivers. The greater residual effect at Call Street than Dogwood Way (i.e., 68% vs. 17.6% in-

creases over initial baseline, respectively) may have been partially due to the more homogeneous and consistent sample of drivers (i.e., only faculty and staff) exiting the electronically gated Call Street lot. Although systematic records were not maintained, observers did note a substantial number of non-decaled and student-decaled vehicles exiting the Dogwood Way lot. Previous safety belt research has demonstrated significant response maintenance advantages when individuals received repeated rewards for being buckled up (Geller, 1983); and other campus-based programs have found faculty and staff to be much more responsive than students to incentives for safety belt use (Geller, Kalsher, Lehman, & Rudd, 1986; Rudd & Geller, 1985).

Rudd and Geller (1985) implemented a campuswide incentive program for safety belt promotion during a consecutive 3-week period within each quarter of the 1983–84 academic year. Each withdrawal phase at the end of the fall, winter, and spring quarters showed increasing residual effects. In other words, when each incentive program was withdrawn, campuswide safety belt use decreased prominently but remained significantly above the pre-intervention baseline of that quarter. And, this stepwise residual effect was greater for faculty and staff than students. Geller et al. (1986)

148

replicated these findings during the 1984–85 academic year with a different incentive approach toward safety belt promotion.

The present study of campus-based prompting showed stepwise residual effects similar to those observed with the application of incentives. However, it is noteworthy that the phase durations were quite short and there was only one withdrawal phase per parking lot. It would certainly be instructive to alternate several baseline and flashing phases over an extended time period. Furthermore, the recording of vehicle license plate numbers would enable a precise evaluation of repeated flashes per individual driver. Future research should also address the necessary components of the flashing intervention. For example, it is likely that the active display and manipulation of the flash card by a flasher was necessary, because in two previous studies, patrons leaving a bank exchange window did not buckle up when handed a flyer that politely requested safety belt use (Geller, Johnson, & Pelton, 1982; Johnson & Geller, 1984).

In summary, the present study demonstrated substantial behavior change potential of a simple prompting technique that could be integrated readily with large-scale education, legal, and incentive approaches to safety belt promotion, and thereby increase the impact of a comprehensive safety belt program. Also, the research raised important empirical questions regarding the long-term, repeated impact of the Flash-for-Life technique. The need for follow-up study is underlined by the simplicity and low cost of this prompting strategy and by the life-saving potential of an intervention that increases the wearing of vehicle safety belts.

NOTES

The authors are grateful for the helpful comments and suggestions by Galen R. Lehman on an earlier draft of this paper.

Requests for reprints should be sent to E. Scott Geller, Department of Psychology, Virginia Tech, Blacksburg, VA 24061.

Requests for "Flash-for-Life" cards for research purposes should be sent to E. Scott Geller at the above address.

REFERENCES

Barlow, D. H., & Hersen, M. (1984). *Single case experimental designs: Strategies for studying behavior change* (2nd ed.). Elmsford, NY: Pergamon Press.

Bigelow, B. E. (1982). The NHTSA Program of Safety Belt Research. *SAE Techincal Paper Series*, No. 820797. Warrendale, PA: Society of Automotive Engineers.

Department of Transportation. (1983, October). Federal motor vehicle safety standards: Occupant crash protection. *Federal Register*, 48(203).

Geller, E. S. (1983). Rewarding safety belt usage at an industrial setting: Tests of treatment generality and response maintenance. *Journal of Applied Behavior Analysis*, 16, 43–56.

Geller, E. S. (1984). Motivating safety belt use with incentives: A critical review of the past and a look to the future. *SAE Technical Paper Series*, No. 840326. Warrendale, PA: Society of Automotive Engineers.

Geller, E. S. (1985). *Corporate safety belt programs*. Blacksburg, VA: Virginia Polytechnic Institute and State University.

Geller, E. S., Bruff, C. D., & Nimmer, J. G. (1985). "Flash for life": Community-based prompting for safety belt promotion. *Journal of Applied Behavior Analysis*, 18, 309–314.

Geller, E. S., Farris, J. C., & Post, D. S. (1973). Prompting a consumer behavior for pollution control. *Journal of Applied Behavior Analysis*, 6, 367–376.

Geller, E. S., Johnson, R. P., & Pelton, S. L. (1982). Community-based interventions for encouraging safety belt use. *American Journal of Community Psychology*, 10, 183–195.

Geller, E. S., Kalsher, M. J., Lehman, G. R., & Rudd, J. R. (1986). *A universitywide safety belt program: Using rewards to motivate a buckle-up commitment.* Manuscript in preparation. Blacksburg, VA: Virginia Polytechnic Institute and State University.

Geller, E. S., Winett, R. A., & Everett, P. B. (1982). *Preserving the environment: New strategies for behavior change.* Elmsford, NY: Pergamon Press.

Geller, E. S., Witmer, J. F., & Orebaugh, A. L. (1976). Instructions as a determinant of paper-disposal behaviors. *Environment and Behavior*, 8, 417–438.

Insurance Institute for Highway Safety. (1985, November). *The highway loss reduction status report*, 20(12).

Johnson, R. P., & Geller, E. S. (1984). Contingent versus noncontingent rewards for promoting seat belt use. *Journal of Community Psychology*, 12, 113–122.

Pabon, Sims, Smith, & Associates, Inc. (1983). *Motivation of employers to encourage their employees to use safety belts: Phase II* (Contract No. DTNH 22-80-C-07439). Washington, DC: National Highway Traffic Safety Administration.

Rudd, J. R., & Geller, E. S. (1985). A university-based incentive program to increase safety belt use: Toward cost-effective institutionalization. *Journal of Applied Behavior Analysis*, 18, 215–226.

Sleet, D. A. (1984). A preventative health orientation in safety belt and child safety seat use. *SAE Technical Paper Series*, No. 840325. Warrendale, PA: Society of Automotive Engineers.

Steed, D. K. (1983, September). *Alcohol and safety belts*. Keynote address to the National Conference on Alcohol Countermeasures and Occupant Protection, Denver, CO.

Streff, F. M., & Geller, E. S. (1986). Strategies for motivating safety belt use: The application of applied behavior analysis. *Health Education Research: Theory and Practice*, 1, 47–59.

Two year study shows decrease in safety belt use. (1980). *Emphasis*, 10(3), 4.

LABORATORY EXERCISE 3: DESIGNING SINGLE-CASE -- BEHAVIOR MODIFICATION OF NOCTURNAL ENURESIS (BEDWETTING)

The purpose of this laboratory exercise is to give you experience in designing a single-case experiment, using one of the designs discussed at the beginning of this Topic.

Enuresis (bedwetting) is a common problem that affects 22% of 5 year olds and 10% of 10 year olds (Teets, 1992). Treatment approaches have included drugs or behavior modification procedures. The use of behavior modification procedures to treat nocturnal enuresis has typically involved use of conditioning methods which include the use of a pad and bell, or pad and shock. When using these procedures the onset of nocturnal micturition is followed by the presentation of shock or the sounding of the bell, which awakens the child. While this is the typical behavioral procedure used, a variety of additional techniques, such as reinforcement of dry nights, have been investigated.

Although the enuretic is most typically associated with nocturnal micturition, it has been demonstrated that he or she also has little bladder control diurnally. Enuretics urinate frequently during the day and cystometrographic records reveal that these individuals have a low bladder capacity with strong urges to urinate at low bladder pressures and volume. Such evidence has suggested to a number of researchers that enuretics do not receive sufficiently strong stimulation from the bladder to awaken the individual during sleep. This deficit has been attributed to a variety of factors, which include inadequate physiological or neural maturations and inadequate learning of micturition patterns.

Regardless of the cause of the low bladder capacity of the enuretics, it has been recommended by a number of researchers that treatment should consist of a program that teaches the enuretic to inhibit urination during the day with the expectation that the effect will generalize to nighttime. Treatment should consist of providing the enuretic with an abundance of fluids and instructing him or her to retain the urine for as long as possible. Such retention is expected to expand the capacity of the bladder to enable one to hold the 10 to 12 oz. of urine required for the output of night urine.

Your task is to design an experiment which will test the effectiveness of this method of retention training conditioning treating enuretics. Write up this laboratory exercise as a methods section, according to APA Publication Manual guidelines.

References:

El-Anany, F. G., Maghraby, H. A., Shaker, S. E., & Abdel-Moneim, A. M. (1999). Primary nocturnal enuresis: a new approach to conditioning treatment. *Urology, 53*, 405-408.

Kaplan, S. L., Breit, M., Gauthier, B., & Busner, J. (1989). A comparison of three nocturnal enuresis treatment methods. *Journal of the American Academy of Child and Adolescent Psychiatry, 28*, 282-286.

Mellon, M. W., & McGrath, M. L. (2000). Empirically supported treatments in pediatric psychology: Nocturnal enuresis. *Journal of Pediatric Psychology, 25*, 193-214.

Ronen, T., Wozner, U., & Rahaw, G. (1992). Cognitive intervention in enuresis. *Child and Family Behavior Therapy, 14*, 1-14.

Scott, M. A., Barclay, D. R., & Houts, A. C. (1992). Childhood enuresis: Etiology, assessment, and current behavioral treatment. *Progress in Behavior Modification, 28*. 83-117.

Teets, J. M. (1992). Enuresis: nursing diagnoses and treatment. *Journal of Community Health Nursing, 9*, 95-101.

LABORATORY EXERCISE 4: DESIGNING SINGLE-CASE STUDY -- BEHAVIOR MODIFICATION OF BIZARRE VERBALIZATIONS

The purpose of this laboratory exercise is to give you experience in designing a single-case experiment, using one of the designs discussed at the beginning of this topic.

In the past it has been recognized that a camp environment may provide an excellent situation for applying behavioral procedures for the remediation of problematic behaviors. Although little research has been conducted in such settings they are considered advantageous from the standpoint of providing a natural setting for conducting controlled research. Additionally, camp environments have the physical facilities and the social environment capable of providing strong reinforcers to children, and the environment is rather novel, which may be conducive to behavior change.

It has just been pointed out that there are many characteristics of a camp setting that make it an excellent environment to administer a behavioral program that remedies problematic behaviors. Assume that, because of lack of systematic evidence to support the above contentions, you wanted to demonstrate the utility of camp settings. Assume further that you had contacted a camp that would allow you to conduct a research study and that they had admitted an 8-year-old minimally brain damaged boy who demonstrated a high frequency of bizarre verbalizations primarily about penguins. Since these verbalizations interfered with his development of good interpersonal relations with adults or peers, you consider him to be an excellent candidate for your study. You decided to use extinction in an attempt to eliminate these bizarre verbalizations in four camp settings: walking on the trail/evening activity, dining hall, cabin, and education. Your task is to design a study that would test the effectiveness of extinction in eliminating these bizarre verbalizations.

Your task is to design a single-case experiment.

Write up this laboratory exercise as a method section, according to APA Publication Manual guidelines.

References:

Konczak, L. J., & Johnson, C. M. (1983). Reducing inappropriate verbalizations in a sheltered workshop through differential reinforcement of other behavior. *Education & Training of the Mentally Retarded, 18*, 120-124.

Vollmer, T. R., Borrero, J. C., Lalli, J. S., & Daniel, D. (1999). Evaluating self-control and impulsivity in children with severe behavior disorders. *Journal of Applied Behavior Analysis, 32*, 451-466.

LABORATORY EXERCISE 5: DESIGNING A SINGLE-GROUP STUDY -- REDUCING LITTERING BEHAVIOR

The purpose of this laboratory exercise is to give you experience in designing an environmental psychology study which uses an A-B-A design.

Environmental psychologists have become interested in determining ways in which we can change behavior of individuals so that they preserve their environments. An excellent book that summarizes many studies in this area was written by Geller, Winett, and Everett (1982).

As you have probably noticed, littering is a problem along some of our highways. You are assigned to develop a project to evaluate a way to make people stop, or at least, decrease their littering behavior. You can either threaten (possible punishment) or reward (positive reinforcement) non-littering behavior through the use of signs, fines, or other methods.

Your task is to design an A-B-A quasi-experimental study which will evaluate the effectiveness of some treatment on littering behavior. Determine where, when, and under what conditions you will conduct your study. What is (are) your independent variable(s)? What is (are) your dependent variables (s)? How will you operationally define "littering"? What is your procedure?

Write up this laboratory exercise as a method section, according to APA Publication Manual guidelines.

References:

Dixon, R. S., & Moore, D. W. (1992). The effects of posted feedback on littering: Another look. *Behaviour Change, 9,* 83-86.

Geller, W. S., Winett, R. A., & Everett, P. B. (1982). *Preserving the environment: New strategies for behavior change.* New York: Pergamon.

Goldstein, A. P. (1996). *The psychology of vandalism.* New York: Plenum Press.

Houghton, S. (1993). Using verbal and visual prompts to control littering in high schools. *Educational Studies, 19,* 247-254.

Keenan, M. (1996). The A, B, C of litter control. *Irish Journal of Psychology, 17,* 327-339.

Levitt, L., & Leventhal, G. (1986). Litter reduction: How effective is the New York State Bottle Bill? *Environment and Behavior, 18,* 467-479.

Meeker, F. L. (1997). A comparison of table-littering behavior in two settings: A case for a contextual research strategy. *Journal of Environmental Education, 17,* 59-68.

Reams, M. A., Geaghan, J. P., & Gendron, R. C. (1996). The link between recycling and litter: A field study. *Environment and Behavior, 28,* 92-110.

Takahashi, N. (1996). A study of litter prevention at a shopping mall. *Japanese Journal of Psychology, 67,* 94-101.

LABORATORY EXERCISE 1: ETHICS OF PSYCHOLOGICAL RESEARCH

The purpose of this laboratory exercise is to help you become more sensitive to ethical issues through the examination of published psychological studies.

You should have read the chapter on ethics in your experimental methods book before proceeding with this assignment. On the Internet, you can access APA's Ethical Principles of Psychologists and Code of Conduct (http://www.apa.org/ethics/code.html) and the Canadian Psychological Association's Canadian Code of Ethics for Psychologists (http://www.cpa.ca/ethics.html). In addition, you may wish to refer to some of the previous references and Internet sites, as well as some of the following:

American Psychological Association (1982). *Ethical principles in the conduct of research with human participants*. Washington, DC: APA.

American Psychological Association (1992). Ethical principles of psychologists. *American Psychologist, 45*, 1597-1611.

Bersoff, D. N. (1999). *Ethical conflicts in psychology* (2nd ed). Washington, DC: APA.

Brabeck, M. M. (2000). *Practicing feminist ethics in psychology*. Washington, DC: APA.

Chastain, G., & Landrum, R. E. (1999). *Protecting human subjects: Departmental subject pools and Institutional Review Boards*. Washington, DC: APA.

Dawkins, M. S., & Gosline, M. (Eds.) (1992). *Ethics in research on animal behaviour: Readings from "Animal Behaviour"* . San Diego, CA: Academic Press.

Foundation for Biomedical Research (1987). *The biomedical investigator's handbook for researchers using animal models*. Washington, DC: Foundation for Biomedical Research.

Nagy, T. F. (1999). *Ethics in plain English: An illustrative casebook for psychologists*. Washington, DC: APA.

NIH (1985). *Guide for the care and use of laboratory animals*. NIH Publication No. 85-23, Revised 1985, Office of Science and Health Reports, DRR/NIH, Bethseda, MD 20205.

National Institutes of Health (1991). *Preparation and maintenance of higher mammals during neuroscience experiments*. NIH Publication No 91-3207. Bethesda, MD; National Eye Institute.

Society for Neuroscience (1991). *Handbook of the use of animals in research*. Washington, DC: Society for Neuroscience.

Sales, B. D., & Folkman, S. (2000). *Ethics in research with human participants*. Washington, DC: APA.

The following articles were selected specifically to illustrate certain ethical issues that confront researchers. The abstract of the article is provided when possible. That these articles were selected does not mean that they have been judged to be unethical, although some researchers have raised questions about some of them since their publication. References to criticisms and rebuttals in the literature are also provided. Please remember that ethical issues are present in any study. Some of these studies were carried out before human participants or animal care rights committees had been formed. In recent years our profession and society, in general, has become much more sensitive to ethical issues.

Your instructor will assign you one of two activities:

(1) Debate on ethics. You will be assigned to debate teams. Your debate team's responsibility will be to read the assigned set of articles. You are to prepare yourselves to argue either that there are or are not ethical problems involved, supporting your arguments with the ethical principles of the American Psychological Association and other sources. Once you have prepared your debate points, your instructor will have groups of students debate each of the assigned sets of research.

(2) Evaluation of ethical issues. You will be assigned articles under one or more of the sets of articles below. You are to write an evaluation of the ethical issues that are raised and the degree to which the rights and welfare of the participants are protected. Indicate how you would resolve any ethical issues (e.g., redesigning the experiment).

ANIMAL RESEARCH:

A. Autonomic nervous system learning

1. DiCara, L. V., & Miller, N. E. (1968). Changes in heart rate instrumental-learned by curarized rats as avoidance responses. *Journal of Comparative and Physiological Psychology, 65*, 8-12.

2 groups of curarized rats learned to increase or decrease, respectively, their heart rates in order to escape or avoid mild electric shocks. Responses in the appropriate direction were greater during the stimulus preceding shock than during control intervals between shock; they change in the opposite direction, toward the initial pretraining level, during the different stimulus preceding nonshock. Electromyograms indicated complete paralysis of the gastrocnemius muscle throughout training and for a period of at least 1 hr. thereafter (p. 8).

2. Di Cari, L. V. (1970). Learning in the autonomic nervous system. *Scientific American, 222*, 30-39.

B. Learned Helplessness

1. Seligman, M. E. P., & Beagley, G. (1975). Learned helplessness in the rat. *Journal of Comparative and Physiological Psychology, 88*, 534-541.

Four experiments attempted to produce behavior in the rat parallel to the behavior characteristic of learned helplessness in the dog. When rats received escapable, inescapable, or no shock and were later tested in jump-up escape, both inescapable and no-shock controls failed to escape. When bar pressing, rather than jumping up, was used as the tested escape response, fixed ratio (FR) 3 was interfered with by inescapable shock, but not lesser ratios. With FR-3, the no-shock control escaped well. Interference with escape was shown to be a function of the inescapability of shock and not shock per se: Rats that were "put through" and learned a prior jump-up escape did not become passive, but their yoked, inescapable partners did. Rats, as well as dogs, fail to escape shock as a function of prior inescapability, exhibiting learned helplessness (p.534).

2. Seligman, M. E. P., & Groves, D. P. (1970). Nontransient learned helplessness. *Psychonomic Science, 19*, 191-192.

Dogs who receive repeated, spaced exposure to inescapable electric shock in a Pavlovian hammock fail to escape shock in a shuttlebox 1 week later, while one session of inescapable shock produces only transient interference. Cage-raised beagles are more susceptible to interference produced by inescapable shock than are mongrels of unknown history. These results are compatible with learned helplessness and contradict the hypothesis that failure to escape shock is produced by transient stress (p. 191).

HUMAN RESEARCH:

A. Portrayals of sexual violence

1. Malamuth, N. M., Heim, M., & Feshbach, S. (1980). Sexual responsiveness of college students to rape depictions: Inhibitory and disinhibitory effects. *Journal of Personality and Social Psychology, 38*, 399-408.

Two experiments were conducted to identify the specific dimensions in portrayals of sexual violence that inhibit or disinhibit the sexual responsiveness of male and female college students. The first experiment replicated earlier findings that normals are less sexually aroused by portrayals of sexual assault than by depictions of mutually consenting sex. In the second experiment, it was shown that portraying the rape victim as experiencing an involuntary orgasm disinhibited subjects' sexual responsiveness and resulted in levels of arousal comparable to those elicited by depictions of mutually consenting sex. Surprisingly, however, it was found that although female subjects were most aroused when the rape victim was portrayed as experiencing an orgasm and no pain, males were most aroused when the victim experienced an orgasm and pain. The relevance of these data to pornography and to the common belief among rapists that their victims derive pleasure from being assaulted is discussed. Misattribution, identification, and power explanations of the findings are also discussed. Finally, it is suggested that arousing stimuli that fuse sexuality and violence may have antisocial effects (p. 399).

2. Sherif, C. W. (1980).Comment on ethical issues in Malamuth, Heim, and Feshbach's "Sexual responsiveness of college students to rape depictions: Inhibitory and disinhibitory effects". *Journal of Personality and Social Psychology, 38*, 409-412.

3. Malamuth, N. M., Feshbach, S., & Heim, M. (1980). Ethical issues and exposure to rape stimuli: A reply to Sherif. *Journal of Personality and Social Psychology, 38*, 413-415.

4. Check, J. V., & Malamuth, N. M. (1984). Can there be positive effects of participation in pornography experiments. *Journal of Sex Research, 20*, 14-31.

Conducted a 2-phase experiment in response to recent ethical concerns about the possible antisocial effects of exposing research Ss to pornographic rape portrayals. In Phase 1, 64 male and 64 female undergraduates were randomly assigned to read either an "acquaintance" or a "stranger" rape depiction, or to read control materials. Ss who read the rape depictions were then given a rape debriefing that included a communication about the undesirable desensitizing effects of pairing sexual violence with other highly explicit and pleasing sexual stimuli. Half of the Ss who read the control materials were also given the rape debriefing. In Phase 2, Ss were presented with a number of newspaper articles in which a newspaper report of a rape was embedded and asked to give their opinions. Results indicate that the rape debriefing generally increased Ss' perceptions of pornography as a cause of rape. Ss in the rape debriefing conditions also gave the rapist in the newspaper report a higher sentence and saw the rape victim as less responsible than did Ss in the control conditions. This latter effect, however, occurred only under conditions where Ss had earlier been exposed to an example of a rape depiction that was relevant to both the rape myths discussed in the rape debriefing and the newspaper report of the rape (p. 14).

B. Participation in a burglary

1. West, S. G., Gunn, S. P., & Chernicky, P. (1975). Ubiquitous Watergate: An attributional analysis. *Journal of Personality and Social Psychology, 32*, 55-65.

Actor-observer differences in causal attribution were investigated in an experiment involving two separate studies. Study 1 was a field experiment in which 80 subjects (actors) were presented with elaborate plans for burglarizing a local advertising firm under one of four experimental conditions: (a) a control condition, (b) $2,000 (reward), (c) government sponsorship but no immunity from prosecution, and (d) government sponsorship plus immunity. In Study 2, 238 subjects (observers) read a description of a student agreeing or refusing to participate in the burglary under one of the four experimental conditions. Consistent with Jones and Nisbett's 1971 theory, actors made more environmental attributions, while observers made more dispositional attributions. Further, observers made more dispositional attributions when the actor agreed than when he refused, except in the reward condition, where this relationship was reversed. The results are interpreted with reference to the disparate explanations of Watergate offered by the Nixon administration and the press (p. 55).

2. Cook, Stuart W. (1975). A comment on the ethical issues involved in West, Gunn, and Chernicky's "Ubiquitous Watergate: An attributional analysis". *Journal of Personality and Social Psychology, 32*, 66-68.

C. Behavioral study of obedience in children

1. Shanab, M. E., & Yahya, K. (1977). A behavioral study of obedience in children. *Journal of Personality and Social Psychology, 35,* 530-536.

Using Milgram's original test of obedience, 192 Jordanian subjects were tested in a 2 X 2 X 3 design in which sex, two kinds of punishment instructions, and three levels of age groups (6-8, 10-12, 14-16 years) were combined factorially. The instructions issued to the experimental group were identical to those used in Milgram's paradigm in that teacher subjects were asked to administer shock to confederate learners each time the latter made a mistake in a paired-associate task and to increase the shock level with each additional mistake. The subjects in the control group were given a free choice of delivering or not delivering shock each time the learner made a mistake. The results showed that 73% of all experimental subjects, as opposed to 16% of the control subjects, continued to deliver shock to the end of the shock scale. Neither age nor sex differences in obedience rate were found. However, significantly more obedient females than males reported that they punished the learners because they were obeying orders (p. 530).

D. Invasion of personal space

1. Middlemist, R. D., Knowles, E. S., & Matter, C. (1976). Personal space invasions in the lavatory: Suggestive evidence for arousal. *Journal of Personality and Social Psychology, 33,* 541-546.

The hypothesis that personal space invasions produce arousal was investigated in a field experiment. A men's lavatory provided a setting where norms for privacy were salient, where personal space invasions could occur in the case of men urinating, where the opportunity for compensatory responses to invasion were minimal, and where proximity-induced arousal could be measured. Research on micturition indicates that social stressors inhibit relaxation of the external urethral sphincter, which would delay the onset of micturition, and that they increase intravesical pressure, which would shorten the duration of micturition once begun. Sixty lavatory users were randomly assigned to one of three levels of interpersonal distance and their micturition times were recorded. In a three-urinal lavatory, a confederate stood immediately adjacent to a subject, one urinal removed, or was absent. Paralleling the results of a correlational pilot study, close interpersonal distances increased the delay of onset and decreased the persistence of micturition. These findings provide objective evidence that personal space invasions produce physiological changes associated with arousal.

E. Treating autism and severe behavior disorders

1. Lovaas, O. I., Schaeffer, B., & Simmons, J. Q. (1965). Experimental studies in childhood schizophrenia: Building social behavior in autistic children by use of electric shock. *Journal of Experimental Research in Personality, 1,* 99-109.

Three experimental investigations were carried out on two five-year-old identical twins diagnosed as childhood schizophrenics by using painful electric shock in an attempt to modify their behaviors. Their autistic features were pronounced; they manifested no social responsiveness, speech, nor appropriate play with objects. They engaged in considerable self-stimulatory behaviors and in bizarre, repetitive bodily movements. They had not responded to traditional treatment effects. The studies show that it was possible to modify their behaviors by the use of electric shock. They learned to approach adults to avoid shock. Shock was effective in eliminating pathological behaviors, such as self-stimulation and tantrums. Affectionate and other social behaviors toward adults increased after adults had been associated with shock reduction.

2. Schopler, E. (1988). Concerns about misinterpretation and uncritical acceptance of exaggerated claims. *American Psychologist, 43,* 658.
3. Lovaas, O. I. (1989). Concerns about misinterpretation and placement of blame. *American Psychologist, 44,* 143-144.

F. **Electroconvulsive therapy**

1. Breeding, J. (2000). Electroshock and informed consent. *Journal of Humanistic Psychology, 40*, 65-79.

Informed consent is a vital issue in all forms of medicine, especially in psychiatry, where patients are often in extremely vulnerable states of mind, customary practice involves high risk to patients, and the law allows for abrogation of traditional civil rights based on judgments of perceived mental incompetence. This article addresses informed consent related to the practice of electroshock. The author argues that genuine informed consent for electroshock is nonexistent because psychiatrists deny or minimize its harmful effects and, as long as the threat--overt or covert--of involuntary treatment exists, there can be no truly voluntary informed consent. The author discusses 4 primary ways psychiatry violates informed consent in electroshock practice and presents an outline of important information to know about electroshock. An annotated review of the research is provided to back up each of the author's assertions about medical effects and lack of efficacy of electroshock.

2. Lisanby, S. H., Maddox, J. H., Prudic, J., Devanand, D. P., & Sackeim, H. A. (2000). The effects of electroconvulsive therapy on memory of autobiographical and public events. *Archives of General Psychiatry, 57*, 581-590.

BACKGROUND: Retrograde amnesia is the most persistent cognitive adverse effect of electroconvulsive therapy (ECT); however, it is not known whether ECT has differential effects on autobiographical vs impersonal memories. This study examined the short- and long-term effects of differing forms of ECT on memory of personal and impersonal (public) events. METHODS: Fifty-five patients with major depression were randomly assigned to right unilateral (RUL) or bilateral (BL) ECT, each at either low or high electrical dosage. The Personal and Impersonal Memory Test was administered by blinded raters at baseline, during the week after ECT, and at the 2-month follow-up. Normal controls were tested at matched intervals. RESULTS: Shortly after ECT, patients recalled fewer events and event details than controls, with the deficits most marked for impersonal compared with personal events. Bilateral ECT caused more marked amnesia for events and details than RUL ECT, and especially for impersonal memories. These effects were independent of electrical dosage and clinical outcome. At the 2-month follow-up, patients had reduced retrograde amnesia, but continued to show deficits in recalling the occurrence of impersonal events and the details of recent impersonal events. CONCLUSIONS: The amnestic effects of ECT are greatest and most persistent for knowledge about the world (impersonal memory), compared with knowledge about the self (personal memory), for recent compared with distinctly remote events, and for less salient events. Bilateral ECT produces more profound amnestic effects than RUL ECT, particularly for memory of impersonal events.

3. Cohen, D., Flament, M., Taieb, O., Thompson, C., & Basquin, M. (2000). Electroconvulsive therapy in adolescence. *European Child and Adolescent Psychiatry, 9*, 1-6.

The aim of this work is to discuss the ethical issues regarding the use of electroconvulsive therapy (ECT) in adolescents. Ethical implications of ECT in adolescents are analyzed in the light of general medical ethics, which include five prominent principles with respect to autonomy, nonmaleficence, beneficence, justice, and cautiousness. As adults, adolescents with acute psychotic impairment raise an inherent conflict between the respect for the patient's autonomy, on the one side, and the principle of beneficence on the other. However, this age group presents particular dilemmas: (i) As any adolescent suffering from a psychiatric illness is a highly vulnerable subject, society asks for particular attention. The consequence of potential overprotection is that the adolescent may remain untreated because of unrealistic fears regarding ETC. (ii) Some of these fears are linked to the cognitive secondary effects of ETC. Although preliminary data are reassuring, more empirical research on this population should be encouraged. (Iii) Cautiousness recommends the use of ECT in limited indications catatonia, mood disorders, and intractable acute psychotic disorders. We conclude that there is no ethical reason to ban the use of ECT in adolescents . . . .

LABORATORY EXERCISE 2: EVALUATING AND DEVELOPING CONSENT FORMS

The purpose of this laboratory exercise is to give you experience in developing informed consent forms.

First read the following examples of informed consent and then develop your own consent form for one of the experiments or surveys you carried out in your class this year, or an experiment you would like to carry out. Obtain the necessary forms and directions from your department's Human Subjects Committee or from the Institutional Review Board. Prepare the consent form as if you were going to present it to an Institutional Review Board for approval. Turn this into your instructor.

Go to the following Internet site to read The Office for Human Research Protections' *Policy and Assurances*: http://ohrp.osophs.dhhs.gov/polasur.htm. Their section on Informed Consent Information, particularly "Tips on Informed Consent" and "Informed Consent Checklist", provides highly relevant information for developing your own consent forms.

Listed below are some research articles that investigated the impact of consent forms on research as well as some articles that address issues surrounding informed consent regulations. Of increasing concern is the development of adequate consent forms for children (Glantz, 1996), the elderly (Cassel, 1987), and special populations (e.g., Appelbaum, Grisso, Frank, O'Donnell, & Kupfer, 1999; Arscott, Dagnan, & Kroese, 1999; Ferraro, Orvedal, & Plaud, 1998; McCrady & Bux, 1999; Roberts, 2000). You may be asked to read one or more, and present a summary to your classmates.

References:

Appelbaum, P. S., Grisso, T., Frank, E., O'Donnell, S., Kupfer, D. J. (1999). Competence of depressed patients for consent to research. *American Journal of Psychiatry, 156*, 1380-1384.

Arscott, K., Dagnan, D., & Kroese, B. S. (1999). Assessing the ability of people with a learning disability to give informed consent for treatment. *Psychological Medicine, 29*, 1367-1375.

Bradley, E. J., & Lindsay, R. C. (1987). Methodological and ethical issues in child abuse research. *Journal of Family Violence, 2*, 239-255.

Cassel, C. K. (1987). Informed consent for research in geriatrics: History and concepts. *Journal of the American Geriatrics Society, 35*, 542-544.

Ferraro, F. R., Orvedal, L., & Plaud, J. J. (1998). Institutional Review Board issues related to special populations. *Journal of General Psychology, 125*, 156-164.

Finney, P. D. (1987). When consent information refers to risk and deception: Implications for social research. *Journal of Social Behavior and Personality, 2*, 37-48.

Glantz, L. H. (1996). Conducting research with children: legal and ethical issues. *Journal of the American Academy of Child and Adolescent Psychiatry, 35*, 1283-1291.

Korn, J. H. (1988). Students' roles, rights, and responsibilities as research participants. *Teaching of Psychology, 15*, 74-78.

Lavelle, J. C., Byrne, D. J., Rice, P., & Cuschieri, A. (1993). Factors affecting quality of informed consent. *British Medical Journal, 306*, 885-890.

McCrady, B. S., & Bux, D. A. (1999). Ethical issues in informed consent with substance abusers. *Journal of Consulting and Clinical Psychology, 67*, 186-193.

Pattullo, E. L. (1987). Exemption from review, not informed consent. *IRB: A Review of Human Subjects Research, 9*, 6-8.

Roberts, L. W. (2000). Evidence-based ethics and informed consent in mental illness research. *Archives of General Psychiatry, 57*, 540-542.

Sieber, J. E., & Saks, M. J. (1989). A census of subject pool characteristics and policies. *American Psychologist, 44*, 1053-1061.

Sieber, J. E., & Stanley, B. (1988). Ethical and professional dimensions of socially sensitive research. *American Psychologist, 43*, 49-55.

Young, D. R., Hooker, D. T., Freeberg, F. E. (1990). Informed consent documents: Increasing comprehension by reducing reading level. *IRB: A Review of Human Subjects Research, 12*, 1-5.

Consent Form for Anonymous Virginia Tech Survey:

Alcohol and Drug Use, and Related Activities

1. Purpose of Survey

This is a *COMPLETELY ANONYMOUS* survey about the attitudes and activities of the general undergraduate student at Virginia Tech on the topics of alcohol and drug usage. It is being conducted by undergraduates in a psychology course that is devoted to learning more about college life. Only if you are an undergraduate at Virginia Tech, aged 18 years or older, are you to participate.

2. Procedure to be followed in Survey

You may examine the survey questionnaire first. You will be asked to answer questions concerning your recent alcohol and other drug usage, as well as general background information. You will mark your responses on an opscan. Some of the questions are personal. *You may skip any question you do not want to answer or you may stop at any time.*

3. ANONYMITY OF PARTICIPANTS AND CONFIDENTIALITY OF RESULTS

This survey is *completely anonymous and you cannot be identified in any way.* You are not to put your name on the questionnaire. To further ensure anonymity, you are to fill out the questionnaire in such a manner that the experimenter cannot see your responses. Finally, you are to place your opscan through a slit in a sealed manila envelope. The student researcher has signed a code of ethics indicating that he/she will not examine the individual response forms that are gathered. The response forms will be gathered all together from the class and submitted to the testing center for transfer to a summary data set.

4. DISCOMFORTS AND RISKS

There are no risks in this survey. If you feel uncomfortable about any of the questions, you may skip them or stop answering the questionnaire at anytime.

5. BENEFITS OF THIS STUDY

Your participation will help us advance knowledge about these topics at Virginia Tech. As part of the class activity, this information will be coded into the computer and then analyzed. We hope to present the results to the Dean of Students at Virginia Tech and to have a summary published in the student newspaper. This data will also be compared with similar questionnaires administered in 1993, 1995, and 1999 at Virginia Tech. A summary of the findings will be available from Dr. Crawford, Psychology Department, in December 1999.

6. FREEDOM TO WITHDRAW

You are free to withdraw from this survey at any time. You may skip any question you do not want to answer.

8. APPROVAL OF RESEARCH

This survey has been approved by the Human Subjects Committee of the Department of Psychology and by the Institutional Review Board of Virginia Tech. All participants involved in this survey will receive a copy of this consent form.

Should you have any questions, please feel free to contact any of the following:

Helen Crawford, Ph.D., Psychology Faculty Supervisor	231-6520
David Harrison, Ph.D., Chair, Human Subjects Committee	231-6581
Tom Hurd, Chair, Institutional Review Board	231-6077

9. PARTICIPANT'S PERMISSION

You have had an opportunity to ask questions and have had them all answered. You realize that this is an anonymous survey. You realize *that you are not to identify yourself in anyway on the questionnaire*. You realize that you may stop the questionnaire at any time. If you agree to participate, please proceed to answer the questionnaire and follow the directions. Remember to remove yourself from the interviewer and your friends so that you answer the questionnaire out of their vision. Place the opscan into the envelope.

CODE OF ETHICS SIGNED BY STUDENT INTERVIEWER

I, _____, agree to follow the ethical guidelines of the American Psychological Association. I will not examine any of the collected questionnaires.

Signed: _____   Date: _____

APPENDIX A

Surveys for Topic 6:

Laboratory Exercise 2: Survey on Alcohol Use (pp. 65-68)

Laboratory Exercise 3: Survey on Eating Disorders (pp. 69-70)

Laboratory Exercise 4: Survey on ESP Attitudes and Experiences (pp. 71-72)

ANONYMOUS SURVEY: ALCOHOL USAGE BY COLLEGE STUDENTS

Gender: ____ male ____ female   Age now: ____   Age at first drink: _____

Year in college: __ freshman   __ sophomore   __ junior   __ senior   __ grad student

Since school started, on the average, how often do you drink alcohol?	Since school started, on the average, how much alcohol do you drink at any one time?
___ every day	___ more than 6 alcoholic drinks
___ at least once a week, not every day	___ 5 - 6 alcoholic drinks
___ at least once a month, not every week	___ 3 - 4 alcoholic drinks
___ more than once a year, less than once a month	___ 1 - 2 alcoholic drinks
___ once a year	___ less than 1 alcoholic drink
___ never	___ I do not drink

Check appropriate responses:

After drinking alcohol, I	Once or more this past year	Prior to this year	Never
had a hangover	_____	_____	_____
felt nauseated or vomited	_____	_____	_____
experienced a blackout where I could not remember incidents or conversations the next day	_____	_____	_____
binged on alcohol for two or more days	_____	_____	_____
drove a car after several drinks of alcohol	_____	_____	_____
was arrested for DUI	_____	_____	_____
went to class after several drinks of alcohol	_____	_____	_____
missed class or work because of drinking or hangover	_____	_____	_____
was criticized for drinking too much	_____	_____	_____
thought I might have a drinking problem	_____	_____	_____
got a lower grade than I would have if I had not drunk	_____	_____	_____
got into a fight	_____	_____	_____
damaged property	_____	_____	_____
got in trouble with the law	_____	_____	_____

ANONYMOUS SURVEY: ALCOHOL USAGE BY COLLEGE STUDENTS

Gender: ____ male ____ female   Age now: ____   Age at first drink: _____

Year in college: __ freshman   __ sophomore   __ junior   __ senior   __ grad student

Since school started, on the average, how often do you drink alcohol?
___ every day
___ at least once a week, not every day
___ at least once a month, not every week
___ more than once a year, less than once a month
___ once a year
___ never

Since school started, on the average, how much alcohol do you drink at any one time?
___ more than 6 alcoholic drinks
___ 5 - 6 alcoholic drinks
___ 3 - 4 alcoholic drinks
___ 1 - 2 alcoholic drinks
___ less than 1 alcoholic drink
___ I do not drink

Check appropriate responses:

After drinking alcohol, I	Once or more this past year	Prior to this year	Never
had a hangover	_____	_____	_____
felt nauseated or vomited	_____	_____	_____
experienced a blackout where I could not remember incidents or conversations the next day	_____	_____	_____
binged on alcohol for two or more days	_____	_____	_____
drove a car after several drinks of alcohol	_____	_____	_____
was arrested for DUI	_____	_____	_____
went to class after several drinks of alcohol	_____	_____	_____
missed class or work because of drinking or hangover	_____	_____	_____
was criticized for drinking too much	_____	_____	_____
thought I might have a drinking problem	_____	_____	_____
got a lower grade than I would have if I had not drunk	_____	_____	_____
got into a fight	_____	_____	_____
damaged property	_____	_____	_____
got in trouble with the law	_____	_____	_____

ANONYMOUS SURVEY: ALCOHOL USAGE BY COLLEGE STUDENTS

Gender: ____ male ____ female   Age now: _____   Age at first drink: _____

Year in college: __ freshman __ sophomore __ junior __ senior __ grad student

Since school started, on the average, how often do you drink alcohol?	Since school started, on the average, how much alcohol do you drink at any one time?	
___ every day	___ more than 6 alcoholic drinks	
___ at least once a week, not every day	___ 5 - 6 alcoholic drinks	
___ at least once a month, not every week	___ 3 - 4 alcoholic drinks	
___ more than once a year, less than once a month	___ 1 - 2 alcoholic drinks	
___ once a year	___ less than 1 alcoholic drink	
___ never	___ I do not drink	

Check appropriate responses:

After drinking alcohol, I	Once or more this past year	Prior to this year	Never
had a hangover	_____	_____	_____
felt nauseated or vomited	_____	_____	_____
experienced a blackout where I could not remember incidents or conversations the next day	_____	_____	_____
binged on alcohol for two or more days	_____	_____	_____
drove a car after several drinks of alcohol	_____	_____	_____
was arrested for DUI	_____	_____	_____
went to class after several drinks of alcohol	_____	_____	_____
missed class or work because of drinking or hangover	_____	_____	_____
was criticized for drinking too much	_____	_____	_____
thought I might have a drinking problem	_____	_____	_____
got a lower grade than I would have if I had not drunk	_____	_____	_____
got into a fight	_____	_____	_____
damaged property	_____	_____	_____
got in trouble with the law	_____	_____	_____

ANONYMOUS SURVEY: ALCOHOL USAGE BY COLLEGE STUDENTS

Gender: ____ male ____ female   Age now: _____   Age at first drink: _____

Year in college: __ freshman __ sophomore __ junior __ senior __ grad student

Since school started, on the average, how often do you drink alcohol?
___ every day
___ at least once a week, not every day
___ at least once a month, not every week
___ more than once a year, less than once a month
___ once a year
___ never

Since school started, on the average, how much alcohol do you drink at any one time?
___ more than 6 alcoholic drinks
___ 5 - 6 alcoholic drinks
___ 3 - 4 alcoholic drinks
___ 1 - 2 alcoholic drinks
___ less than 1 alcoholic drink
___ I do not drink

Check appropriate responses:

After drinking alcohol, I	Once or more this past year	Prior to this year	Never
had a hangover	_____	_____	_____
felt nauseated or vomited	_____	_____	_____
experienced a blackout where I could not remember incidents or conversations the next day	_____	_____	_____
binged on alcohol for two or more days	_____	_____	_____
drove a car after several drinks of alcohol	_____	_____	_____
was arrested for DUI	_____	_____	_____
went to class after several drinks of alcohol	_____	_____	_____
missed class or work because of drinking or hangover	_____	_____	_____
was criticized for drinking too much	_____	_____	_____
thought I might have a drinking problem	_____	_____	_____
got a lower grade than I would have if I had not drunk	_____	_____	_____
got into a fight	_____	_____	_____
damaged property	_____	_____	_____
got in trouble with the law	_____	_____	_____

ANONYMOUS SURVEY: ALCOHOL USAGE BY COLLEGE STUDENTS

Gender: ___ male ___ female   Age now: _____   Age at first drink: _____

Year in college: __ freshman   __ sophomore   __ junior   __ senior   __ grad student

Since school started, on the average, how often do you drink alcohol?
___ every day
___ at least once a week, not every day
___ at least once a month, not every week
___ more than once a year, less than once a month
___ once a year
___ never

Since school started, on the average, how much alcohol do you drink at any one time?
___ more than 6 alcoholic drinks
___ 5 - 6 alcoholic drinks
___ 3 - 4 alcoholic drinks
___ 1 - 2 alcoholic drinks
___ less than 1 alcoholic drink
___ I do not drink

Check appropriate responses:

After drinking alcohol, I	Once or more this past year	Prior to this year	Never
had a hangover	_____	_____	_____
felt nauseated or vomited	_____	_____	_____
experienced a blackout where I could not remember incidents or conversations the next day	_____	_____	_____
binged on alcohol for two or more days	_____	_____	_____
drove a car after several drinks of alcohol	_____	_____	_____
was arrested for DUI	_____	_____	_____
went to class after several drinks of alcohol	_____	_____	_____
missed class or work because of drinking or hangover	_____	_____	_____
was criticized for drinking too much	_____	_____	_____
thought I might have a drinking problem	_____	_____	_____
got a lower grade than I would have if I had not drunk	_____	_____	_____
got into a fight	_____	_____	_____
damaged property	_____	_____	_____
got in trouble with the law	_____	_____	_____

THE BULIT-R[1]

Answer each question by circling the appropriate answer. Please respond to each item as honestly as possible; remember all of the information you provide is anonymous.

1. I am satisfied with my eating patterns.
    a. agree
    b. neutral
    c. disagree a little
    d. disagree
    e. disagree strongly

2. Would you presently call yourself a "binge eater"?
    a. yes, absolutely
    b. yes
    c. yes, probably
    d. yes, possibly
    e. no, probably not

3. Do you feel you have control over the amount of food you consume?
    a. most or all of the time
    b. a lot of the time
    c. occasionally
    d. rarely
    e. never

4. I am satisfied with the shape and size of my body.
    a. frequently or always
    b. sometimes
    c. occasionally
    d. rarely
    e. seldom or never

5. When I feel that my eating behavior is out of control, I try to take rather extreme measures to get back on course (strict dieting, fasting, laxatives, diuretics, self-induced vomiting, or vigorous exercise).
    a. always
    b. almost always
    c. frequently
    d. sometimes
    e. never or my eating behavior is never out of control

6. I am obsessed about the size and shape of my body.
    a. always
    b. almost always
    c. frequently
    d. sometimes
    e. seldom or never

7. There are times when I rapidly eat a very large amount of food.
    a. more than twice a week
    b. twice a week
    c. once a week
    d. 2-3 times a month
    e. once a month or less (or never)

---

[1]Revised with permission of M. Thelen.

8. How long have you been binge eating (eating uncontrollably to the point of stuffing yourself)?
    a. not applicable; I don't binge eat
    b. less than 3 months
    c. 3 months - 1 year
    d. 1 - 3 years
    e. 3 or more years

9. Most people I know would be amazed if they knew how much food I can consume at one sitting.
    a. without a doubt
    b. very probably
    c. probably
    d. possibly
    e. no

10. Compared with others your age, how preoccupied are you about your weight and body shape?
    a. a great deal more than average
    b. much more than average
    c. more than average
    d. a little more than average
    e. average or less than average

11. I am afraid to eat anything for fear that I won't be able to stop.
    a. always
    b. almost always
    c. frequently
    d. sometimes
    e. seldom or never

12. I feel tormented by the idea that I am fat or might gain weight.
    a. always
    b. almost always
    c. frequently
    d. sometimes
    e. seldom or never

13. How often do you intentionally vomit after eating?
    a. 2 or more times a week
    b. once a week
    c. 2-3 times a month
    d. once a month
    e. less than once a month or never

14. I eat a lot of food when I'm not even hungry.
    a. very frequently
    b. frequently
    c. occasionally
    d. sometimes
    e. seldom or never

15. My eating patterns are different from the eating patterns of most people.
    a. always
    b. almost always
    c. frequently
    d. sometimes
    e. seldom or never

16. After I binge eat I turn to one of several strict methods to try to keep from gaining weight (vigorous exercise, strict dieting, fasting, self-induced vomiting, laxatives, or diuretics).
    a. never or I don't binge eat
    b. rarely
    c. occasionally
    d. a lot of the time
    e. most or all of the time

17. When engaged in an eating binge, I tend to eat foods that are high in carbohydrates (sweets and starches).
    a. always
    b. almost always
    c. frequently
    d. sometimes
    e. seldom, or I don't binge

18. Compared to most people, my ability to control my eating behavior seems to be:
    a. greater than others' ability
    b. about the same
    c. less
    d. much less
    e. I have absolutely no control

19. I would presently label myself a 'compulsive eater' (one who engages in episodes of uncontrolled eating).
    a. absolutely
    b. yes
    c. yes, probably
    d. yes, possibly
    e. no, probably not

20. I hate the way my body looks after I eat too much.
    a. seldom or never
    b. sometimes
    c. frequently
    d. almost always
    e. always

21. When I am trying to keep from gaining weight, I feel that I have to resort to vigorous exercise, strict dieting, fasting, self-induced vomiting, laxatives, or diuretics.
    a. never
    b. rarely
    c. occasionally
    d. a lot of the time
    e. most of all of the time

22. Do you believe that it is easier for you to vomit than it is for most people?
    a. yes, it's no problem at all for me
    b. yes, it's easier
    c. yes, it's a little easier
    d. about the same
    e. no, it's less easy

23. I feel that food controls my life.
    a. always
    b. almost always
    c. frequently
    d. sometimes
    e. seldom or never

24. When consuming a large quantity of food, at what rate of speed do you usually eat?
    a. more rapidly than most people have ever eaten in their lives
    b. a lot more rapidly than most people
    c. a little more rapidly than most people
    d. about the same rate as most people
    e. more slowly than most people (or not applicable)

25. Right after I binge eat I feel:
    a. so fat and bloated I can't stand it
    b. extremely fat
    c. fat
    d. a little fat
    e. OK about how my body looks or I never binge eat

26. Compared to other people of my sex, my ability to always feel in control of how much I eat is:
    a. about the same or greater
    b. a little less
    c. less
    d. much less
    e. a great deal less

27. In the last 3 months, on the average how often did you binge eat (eat uncontrollably to the point of stuffing yourself)?
    a. once a month or less (or never)
    b. 2-3 times a month
    c. once a week
    d. twice a week
    e. more than twice a week

28. Most people I know would be surprised at how fat I look after I eat a lot of food.
    a. yes, definitely
    b. yes
    c. yes, probably
    d. yes, possibly
    e. no, probably not or I never eat a lot of food

29. What gender are you?
    a. male
    b. female

30. What age are you?
    a. Under 18
    b. 18 - 20
    c. 21 - 25
    d. 26 or older

THE BULIT-R[2]

Answer each question by circling the appropriate answer. Please respond to each item as honestly as possible; remember all of the information you provide is anonymous.

1. I am satisfied with my eating patterns.
   a. agree
   b. neutral
   c. disagree a little
   d. disagree
   e. disagree strongly

2. Would you presently call yourself a "binge eater"?
   a. yes, absolutely
   b. yes
   c. yes, probably
   d. yes, possibly
   e. no, probably not

3. Do you feel you have control over the amount of food you consume?
   a. most or all of the time
   b. a lot of the time
   c. occasionally
   d. rarely
   e. never

4. I am satisfied with the shape and size of my body.
   a. frequently or always
   b. sometimes
   c. occasionally
   d. rarely
   e. seldom or never

5. When I feel that my eating behavior is out of control, I try to take rather extreme measures to get back on course (strict dieting, fasting, laxatives, diuretics, self-induced vomiting, or vigorous exercise).
   a. always
   b. almost always
   c. frequently
   d. sometimes
   e. never or my eating behavior is never out of control

6. I am obsessed about the size and shape of my body.
   a. always
   b. almost always
   c. frequently
   d. sometimes
   e. seldom or never

7. There are times when I rapidly eat a very large amount of food.
   a. more than twice a week
   b. twice a week
   c. once a week
   d. 2-3 times a month
   e. once a month or less (or never)

---

[2]Revised with permission of M. Thelen.

8. How long have you been binge eating (eating uncontrollably to the point of stuffing yourself)?
    a. not applicable; I don't binge eat
    b. less than 3 months
    c. 3 months - 1 year
    d. 1 - 3 years
    e. 3 or more years

9. Most people I know would be amazed if they knew how much food I can consume at one sitting.
    a. without a doubt
    b. very probably
    c. probably
    d. possibly
    e. no

10. Compared with others your age, how preoccupied are you about your weight and body shape?
    a. a great deal more than average
    b. much more than average
    c. more than average
    d. a little more than average
    e. average or less than average

11. I am afraid to eat anything for fear that I won't be able to stop.
    a. always
    b. almost always
    c. frequently
    d. sometimes
    e. seldom or never

12. I feel tormented by the idea that I am fat or might gain weight.
    a. always
    b. almost always
    c. frequently
    d. sometimes
    e. seldom or never

13. How often do you intentionally vomit after eating?
    a. 2 or more times a week
    b. once a week
    c. 2-3 times a month
    d. once a month
    e. less than once a month or never

14. I eat a lot of food when I'm not even hungry.
    a. very frequently
    b. frequently
    c. occasionally
    d. sometimes
    e. seldom or never

15. My eating patterns are different from the eating patterns of most people.
    a. always
    b. almost always
    c. frequently
    d. sometimes
    e. seldom or never

16. After I binge eat I turn to one of several strict methods to try to keep from gaining weight (vigorous exercise, strict dieting, fasting, self-induced vomiting, laxatives, or diuretics).
    a. never or I don't binge eat
    b. rarely
    c. occasionally
    d. a lot of the time
    e. most or all of the time

17. When engaged in an eating binge, I tend to eat foods that are high in carbohydrates (sweets and starches).
    a. always
    b. almost always
    c. frequently
    d. sometimes
    e. seldom, or I don't binge

18. Compared to most people, my ability to control my eating behavior seems to be:
    a. greater than others' ability
    b. about the same
    c. less
    d. much less
    e. I have absolutely no control

19. I would presently label myself a 'compulsive eater' (one who engages in episodes of uncontrolled eating).
    a. absolutely
    b. yes
    c. yes, probably
    d. yes, possibly
    e. no, probably not

20. I hate the way my body looks after I eat too much.
    a. seldom or never
    b. sometimes
    c. frequently
    d. almost always
    e. always

21. When I am trying to keep from gaining weight, I feel that I have to resort to vigorous exercise, strict dieting, fasting, self-induced vomiting, laxatives, or diuretics.
    a. never
    b. rarely
    c. occasionally
    d. a lot of the time
    e. most of all of the time

22. Do you believe that it is easier for you to vomit than it is for most people?
    a. yes, it's no problem at all for me
    b. yes, it's easier
    c. yes, it's a little easier
    d. about the same
    e. no, it's less easy

23. I feel that food controls my life.
    a. always
    b. almost always
    c. frequently
    d. sometimes
    e. seldom or never

24. When consuming a large quantity of food, at what rate of speed do you usually eat?
    a. more rapidly than most people have ever eaten in their lives
    b. a lot more rapidly than most people
    c. a little more rapidly than most people
    d. about the same rate as most people
    e. more slowly than most people (or not applicable)

25. Right after I binge eat I feel:
    a. so fat and bloated I can't stand it
    b. extremely fat
    c. fat
    d. a little fat
    e. OK about how my body looks or I never binge eat

26. Compared to other people of my sex, my ability to always feel in control of how much I eat is:
    a. about the same or greater
    b. a little less
    c. less
    d. much less
    e. a great deal less

27. In the last 3 months, on the average how often did you binge eat (eat uncontrollably to the point of stuffing yourself)?
    a. once a month or less (or never)
    b. 2-3 times a month
    c. once a week
    d. twice a week
    e. more than twice a week

28. Most people I know would be surprised at how fat I look after I eat a lot of food.
    a. yes, definitely
    b. yes
    c. yes, probably
    d. yes, possibly
    e. no, probably not or I never eat a lot of food

29. What gender are you?
    a. male
    b. female

30. What age are you?
    a. Under 18
    b. 18 - 20
    c. 21 - 25
    d. 26 or older

THE BULIT-R[3]

Answer each question by circling the appropriate answer. Please respond to each item as honestly as possible; remember all of the information you provide is anonymous.

1. I am satisfied with my eating patterns.
   a. agree
   b. neutral
   c. disagree a little
   d. disagree
   e. disagree strongly

2. Would you presently call yourself a "binge eater"?
   a. yes, absolutely
   b. yes
   c. yes, probably
   d. yes, possibly
   e. no, probably not

3. Do you feel you have control over the amount of food you consume?
   a. most or all of the time
   b. a lot of the time
   c. occasionally
   d. rarely
   e. never

4. I am satisfied with the shape and size of my body.
   a. frequently or always
   b. sometimes
   c. occasionally
   d. rarely
   e. seldom or never

5. When I feel that my eating behavior is out of control, I try to take rather extreme measures to get back on course (strict dieting, fasting, laxatives, diuretics, self-induced vomiting, or vigorous exercise).
   a. always
   b. almost always
   c. frequently
   d. sometimes
   e. never or my eating behavior is never out of control

6. I am obsessed about the size and shape of my body.
   a. always
   b. almost always
   c. frequently
   d. sometimes
   e. seldom or never

7. There are times when I rapidly eat a very large amount of food.
   a. more than twice a week
   b. twice a week
   c. once a week
   d. 2-3 times a month
   e. once a month or less (or never)

---

[3]Revised with permission of M. Thelen.

8. How long have you been binge eating (eating uncontrollably to the point of stuffing yourself)?
   a. not applicable; I don't binge eat
   b. less than 3 months
   c. 3 months - 1 year
   d. 1 - 3 years
   e. 3 or more years

9. Most people I know would be amazed if they knew how much food I can consume at one sitting.
   a. without a doubt
   b. very probably
   c. probably
   d. possibly
   e. no

10. Compared with others your age, how preoccupied are you about your weight and body shape?
    a. a great deal more than average
    b. much more than average
    c. more than average
    d. a little more than average
    e. average or less than average

11. I am afraid to eat anything for fear that I won't be able to stop.
    a. always
    b. almost always
    c. frequently
    d. sometimes
    e. seldom or never

12. I feel tormented by the idea that I am fat or might gain weight.
    a. always
    b. almost always
    c. frequently
    d. sometimes
    e. seldom or never

13. How often do you intentionally vomit after eating?
    a. 2 or more times a week
    b. once a week
    c. 2-3 times a month
    d. once a month
    e. less than once a month or never

14. I eat a lot of food when I'm not even hungry.
    a. very frequently
    b. frequently
    c. occasionally
    d. sometimes
    e. seldom or never

15. My eating patterns are different from the eating patterns of most people.
    a. always
    b. almost always
    c. frequently
    d. sometimes
    e. seldom or never

16. After I binge eat I turn to one of several strict methods to try to keep from gaining weight (vigorous exercise, strict dieting, fasting, self-induced vomiting, laxatives, or diuretics).
    a. never or I don't binge eat
    b. rarely
    c. occasionally
    d. a lot of the time
    e. most or all of the time

17. When engaged in an eating binge, I tend to eat foods that are high in carbohydrates (sweets and starches).
    a. always
    b. almost always
    c. frequently
    d. sometimes
    e. seldom, or I don't binge

18. Compared to most people, my ability to control my eating behavior seems to be:
    a. greater than others' ability
    b. about the same
    c. less
    d. much less
    e. I have absolutely no control

19. I would presently label myself a 'compulsive eater' (one who engages in episodes of uncontrolled eating).
    a. absolutely
    b. yes
    c. yes, probably
    d. yes, possibly
    e. no, probably not

20. I hate the way my body looks after I eat too much.
    a. seldom or never
    b. sometimes
    c. frequently
    d. almost always
    e. always

21. When I am trying to keep from gaining weight, I feel that I have to resort to vigorous exercise, strict dieting, fasting, self-induced vomiting, laxatives, or diuretics.
    a. never
    b. rarely
    c. occasionally
    d. a lot of the time
    e. most of all of the time

22. Do you believe that it is easier for you to vomit than it is for most people?
    a. yes, it's no problem at all for me
    b. yes, it's easier
    c. yes, it's a little easier
    d. about the same
    e. no, it's less easy

23. I feel that food controls my life.
    a. always
    b. almost always
    c. frequently
    d. sometimes
    e. seldom or never

24. When consuming a large quantity of food, at what rate of speed do you usually eat?
    a. more rapidly than most people have ever eaten in their lives
    b. a lot more rapidly than most people
    c. a little more rapidly than most people
    d. about the same rate as most people
    e. more slowly than most people (or not applicable)

25. Right after I binge eat I feel:
    a. so fat and bloated I can't stand it
    b. extremely fat
    c. fat
    d. a little fat
    e. OK about how my body looks or I never binge eat

26. Compared to other people of my sex, my ability to always feel in control of how much I eat is:
    a. about the same or greater
    b. a little less
    c. less
    d. much less
    e. a great deal less

27. In the last 3 months, on the average how often did you binge eat (eat uncontrollably to the point of stuffing yourself)?
    a. once a month or less (or never)
    b. 2-3 times a month
    c. once a week
    d. twice a week
    e. more than twice a week

28. Most people I know would be surprised at how fat I look after I eat a lot of food.
    a. yes, definitely
    b. yes
    c. yes, probably
    d. yes, possibly
    e. no, probably not or I never eat a lot of food

29. What gender are you?
    a. male
    b. female

30. What age are you?
    a. Under 18
    b. 18 - 20
    c. 21 - 25
    d. 26 or older

THE BULIT-R[4]

Answer each question by circling the appropriate answer. Please respond to each item as honestly as possible; remember all of the information you provide is anonymous.

1. I am satisfied with my eating patterns.
   a. agree
   b. neutral
   c. disagree a little
   d. disagree
   e. disagree strongly

2. Would you presently call yourself a "binge eater"?
   a. yes, absolutely
   b. yes
   c. yes, probably
   d. yes, possibly
   e. no, probably not

3. Do you feel you have control over the amount of food you consume?
   a. most or all of the time
   b. a lot of the time
   c. occasionally
   d. rarely
   e. never

4. I am satisfied with the shape and size of my body.
   a. frequently or always
   b. sometimes
   c. occasionally
   d. rarely
   e. seldom or never

5. When I feel that my eating behavior is out of control, I try to take rather extreme measures to get back on course (strict dieting, fasting, laxatives, diuretics, self-induced vomiting, or vigorous exercise).
   a. always
   b. almost always
   c. frequently
   d. sometimes
   e. never or my eating behavior is never out of control

6. I am obsessed about the size and shape of my body.
   a. always
   b. almost always
   c. frequently
   d. sometimes
   e. seldom or never

7. There are times when I rapidly eat a very large amount of food.
   a. more than twice a week
   b. twice a week
   c. once a week
   d. 2-3 times a month
   e. once a month or less (or never)

---

[4]Revised with permission of M. Thelen.

8. How long have you been binge eating (eating uncontrollably to the point of stuffing yourself)?
   a. not applicable; I don't binge eat
   b. less than 3 months
   c. 3 months - 1 year
   d. 1 - 3 years
   e. 3 or more years

9. Most people I know would be amazed if they knew how much food I can consume at one sitting.
   a. without a doubt
   b. very probably
   c. probably
   d. possibly
   e. no

10. Compared with others your age, how preoccupied are you about your weight and body shape?
    a. a great deal more than average
    b. much more than average
    c. more than average
    d. a little more than average
    e. average or less than average

11. I am afraid to eat anything for fear that I won't be able to stop.
    a. always
    b. almost always
    c. frequently
    d. sometimes
    e. seldom or never

12. I feel tormented by the idea that I am fat or might gain weight.
    a. always
    b. almost always
    c. frequently
    d. sometimes
    e. seldom or never

13. How often do you intentionally vomit after eating?
    a. 2 or more times a week
    b. once a week
    c. 2-3 times a month
    d. once a month
    e. less than once a month or never

14. I eat a lot of food when I'm not even hungry.
    a. very frequently
    b. frequently
    c. occasionally
    d. sometimes
    e. seldom or never

15. My eating patterns are different from the eating patterns of most people.
    a. always
    b. almost always
    c. frequently
    d. sometimes
    e. seldom or never

16. After I binge eat I turn to one of several strict methods to try to keep from gaining weight (vigorous exercise, strict dieting, fasting, self-induced vomiting, laxatives, or diuretics).
    a. never or I don't binge eat
    b. rarely
    c. occasionally
    d. a lot of the time
    e. most or all of the time

17. When engaged in an eating binge, I tend to eat foods that are high in carbohydrates (sweets and starches).
    a. always
    b. almost always
    c. frequently
    d. sometimes
    e. seldom, or I don't binge

18. Compared to most people, my ability to control my eating behavior seems to be:
    a. greater than others' ability
    b. about the same
    c. less
    d. much less
    e. I have absolutely no control

19. I would presently label myself a 'compulsive eater' (one who engages in episodes of uncontrolled eating).
    a. absolutely
    b. yes
    c. yes, probably
    d. yes, possibly
    e. no, probably not

20. I hate the way my body looks after I eat too much.
    a. seldom or never
    b. sometimes
    c. frequently
    d. almost always
    e. always

21. When I am trying to keep from gaining weight, I feel that I have to resort to vigorous exercise, strict dieting, fasting, self-induced vomiting, laxatives, or diuretics.
    a. never
    b. rarely
    c. occasionally
    d. a lot of the time
    e. most of all of the time

22. Do you believe that it is easier for you to vomit than it is for most people?
    a. yes, it's no problem at all for me
    b. yes, it's easier
    c. yes, it's a little easier
    d. about the same
    e. no, it's less easy

23. I feel that food controls my life.
    a. always
    b. almost always
    c. frequently
    d. sometimes
    e. seldom or never

24. When consuming a large quantity of food, at what rate of speed do you usually eat?
    a. more rapidly than most people have ever eaten in their lives
    b. a lot more rapidly than most people
    c. a little more rapidly than most people
    d. about the same rate as most people
    e. more slowly than most people (or not applicable)

25. Right after I binge eat I feel:
    a. so fat and bloated I can't stand it
    b. extremely fat
    c. fat
    d. a little fat
    e. OK about how my body looks or I never binge eat

26. Compared to other people of my sex, my ability to always feel in control of how much I eat is:
    a. about the same or greater
    b. a little less
    c. less
    d. much less
    e. a great deal less

27. In the last 3 months, on the average how often did you binge eat (eat uncontrollably to the point of stuffing yourself)?
    a. once a month or less (or never)
    b. 2-3 times a month
    c. once a week
    d. twice a week
    e. more than twice a week

28. Most people I know would be surprised at how fat I look after I eat a lot of food.
    a. yes, definitely
    b. yes
    c. yes, probably
    d. yes, possibly
    e. no, probably not or I never eat a lot of food

29. What gender are you?
    a. male
    b. female

30. What age are you?
    a. Under 18
    b. 18 - 20
    c. 21 - 25
    d. 26 or older

THE BULIT-R[5]

Answer each question by circling the appropriate answer. Please respond to each item as honestly as possible; remember all of the information you provide is anonymous.

1. I am satisfied with my eating patterns.
    a. agree
    b. neutral
    c. disagree a little
    d. disagree
    e. disagree strongly

2. Would you presently call yourself a "binge eater"?
    a. yes, absolutely
    b. yes
    c. yes, probably
    d. yes, possibly
    e. no, probably not

3. Do you feel you have control over the amount of food you consume?
    a. most or all of the time
    b. a lot of the time
    c. occasionally
    d. rarely
    e. never

4. I am satisfied with the shape and size of my body.
    a. frequently or always
    b. sometimes
    c. occasionally
    d. rarely
    e. seldom or never

5. When I feel that my eating behavior is out of control, I try to take rather extreme measures to get back on course (strict dieting, fasting, laxatives, diuretics, self-induced vomiting, or vigorous exercise).
    a. always
    b. almost always
    c. frequently
    d. sometimes
    e. never or my eating behavior is never out of control

6. I am obsessed about the size and shape of my body.
    a. always
    b. almost always
    c. frequently
    d. sometimes
    e. seldom or never

7. There are times when I rapidly eat a very large amount of food.
    a. more than twice a week
    b. twice a week
    c. once a week
    d. 2-3 times a month
    e. once a month or less (or never)

---

[5]Revised with permission of M. Thelen.

8. How long have you been binge eating (eating uncontrollably to the point of stuffing yourself)?
   a. not applicable; I don't binge eat
   b. less than 3 months
   c. 3 months - 1 year
   d. 1 - 3 years
   e. 3 or more years

9. Most people I know would be amazed if they knew how much food I can consume at one sitting.
   a. without a doubt
   b. very probably
   c. probably
   d. possibly
   e. no

10. Compared with others your age, how preoccupied are you about your weight and body shape?
    a. a great deal more than average
    b. much more than average
    c. more than average
    d. a little more than average
    e. average or less than average

11. I am afraid to eat anything for fear that I won't be able to stop.
    a. always
    b. almost always
    c. frequently
    d. sometimes
    e. seldom or never

12. I feel tormented by the idea that I am fat or might gain weight.
    a. always
    b. almost always
    c. frequently
    d. sometimes
    e. seldom or never

13. How often do you intentionally vomit after eating?
    a. 2 or more times a week
    b. once a week
    c. 2-3 times a month
    d. once a month
    e. less than once a month or never

14. I eat a lot of food when I'm not even hungry.
    a. very frequently
    b. frequently
    c. occasionally
    d. sometimes
    e. seldom or never

15. My eating patterns are different from the eating patterns of most people.
    a. always
    b. almost always
    c. frequently
    d. sometimes
    e. seldom or never

16. After I binge eat I turn to one of several strict methods to try to keep from gaining weight (vigorous exercise, strict dieting, fasting, self-induced vomiting, laxatives, or diuretics).
    a. never or I don't binge eat
    b. rarely
    c. occasionally
    d. a lot of the time
    e. most or all of the time

17. When engaged in an eating binge, I tend to eat foods that are high in carbohydrates (sweets and starches).
    a. always
    b. almost always
    c. frequently
    d. sometimes
    e. seldom, or I don't binge

18. Compared to most people, my ability to control my eating behavior seems to be:
    a. greater than others' ability
    b. about the same
    c. less
    d. much less
    e. I have absolutely no control

19. I would presently label myself a 'compulsive eater' (one who engages in episodes of uncontrolled eating).
    a. absolutely
    b. yes
    c. yes, probably
    d. yes, possibly
    e. no, probably not

20. I hate the way my body looks after I eat too much.
    a. seldom or never
    b. sometimes
    c. frequently
    d. almost always
    e. always

21. When I am trying to keep from gaining weight, I feel that I have to resort to vigorous exercise, strict dieting, fasting, self-induced vomiting, laxatives, or diuretics.
    a. never
    b. rarely
    c. occasionally
    d. a lot of the time
    e. most of all of the time

22. Do you believe that it is easier for you to vomit than it is for most people?
    a. yes, it's no problem at all for me
    b. yes, it's easier
    c. yes, it's a little easier
    d. about the same
    e. no, it's less easy

23. I feel that food controls my life.
    a. always
    b. almost always
    c. frequently
    d. sometimes
    e. seldom or never

24. When consuming a large quantity of food, at what rate of speed do you usually eat?
    a. more rapidly than most people have ever eaten in their lives
    b. a lot more rapidly than most people
    c. a little more rapidly than most people
    d. about the same rate as most people
    e. more slowly than most people (or not applicable)

25. Right after I binge eat I feel:
    a. so fat and bloated I can't stand it
    b. extremely fat
    c. fat
    d. a little fat
    e. OK about how my body looks or I never binge eat

26. Compared to other people of my sex, my ability to always feel in control of how much I eat is:
    a. about the same or greater
    b. a little less
    c. less
    d. much less
    e. a great deal less

27. In the last 3 months, on the average how often did you binge eat (eat uncontrollably to the point of stuffing yourself)?
    a. once a month or less (or never)
    b. 2-3 times a month
    c. once a week
    d. twice a week
    e. more than twice a week

28. Most people I know would be surprised at how fat I look after I eat a lot of food.
    a. yes, definitely
    b. yes
    c. yes, probably
    d. yes, possibly
    e. no, probably not or I never eat a lot of food

29. What gender are you?
    a. male
    b. female

30. What age are you?
    a. Under 18
    b. 18 - 20
    c. 21 - 25
    d. 26 or older

EXTRASENSORY PERCEPTION (ESP) SURVEY

This is an anonymous survey, conducted as a project for a course in research methods, about your attitudes toward extrasensory perception (ESP) and whether you have had any ESP experiences.

Please check "yes" or "no" to each of the following statements. If you are unsure, check "no". Do not leave any blank.

		Yes	No
1.	I believe in the existence of ESP.	___	___
2.	I believe I have had at least one ESP experience.	___	___
3.	I believe ghosts exist.	___	___
4.	I believe in life after death.	___	___
5.	I believe that some people can contact people who have died.	___	___
6.	I believe that there are flying saucers and people from other places than earth visiting our planet.	___	___
7.	I have had a telepathic experience, where I felt like I was reading another person's thoughts.	___	___
8.	I have had a specific dream about something which matched in detail an event which occurred after my dream. I did not know about the event at the time of the dream and did not expect it.	___	___
9.	I have had the experience of feeling that "I" was outside of or away from my body. This is called an out-of-body experience or astral projection.	___	___
10.	I have seen, heard, or been touched by another being, often referred to as a ghost, and could not explain the experience as being due to a physical or natural cause.	___	___
11.	I have moved an object with my thoughts alone. This is called psychokinesis (PK).	___	___
12.	I have seen light around the body or body parts of another person. As far as I could tell this was not due to a physical or natural cause. This experience is called an aura.	___	___

Demographic Information:

AGE: _____   GENDER: MALE: _____   FEMALE: _____

EXTRASENSORY PERCEPTION (ESP) SURVEY

This is an anonymous survey, conducted as a project for a course in research methods, about your attitudes toward extrasensory perception (ESP) and whether you have had any ESP experiences.

Please check "yes" or "no" to each of the following statements. If you are unsure, check "no". Do not leave any blank.

	Yes	No
1. I believe in the existence of ESP.	___	___
2. I believe I have had at least one ESP experience.	___	___
3. I believe ghosts exist.	___	___
4. I believe in life after death.	___	___
5. I believe that some people can contact people who have died.	___	___
6. I believe that there are flying saucers and people from other places than earth visiting our planet.	___	___
7. I have had a telepathic experience, where I felt like I was reading another person's thoughts.	___	___
8. I have had a specific dream about something which matched in detail an event which occurred after my dream. I did not know about the event at the time of the dream and did not expect it.	___	___
9. I have had the experience of feeling that "I" was outside of or away from my body. This is called an out-of-body experience or astral projection.	___	___
10. I have seen, heard, or been touched by another being, often referred to as a ghost, and could not explain the experience as being due to a physical or natural cause.	___	___
11. I have moved an object with my thoughts alone. This is called psychokinesis (PK).	___	___
12. I have seen light around the body or body parts of another person. As far as I could tell this was not due to a physical or natural cause. This experience is called an aura.	___	___

Demographic Information:

AGE: _____   GENDER: MALE: _____   FEMALE: _____

EXTRASENSORY PERCEPTION (ESP) SURVEY

This is an anonymous survey, conducted as a project for a course in research methods, about your attitudes toward extrasensory perception (ESP) and whether you have had any ESP experiences.

Please check "yes" or "no" to each of the following statements. If you are unsure, check "no". Do not leave any blank.

		Yes	No
1.	I believe in the existence of ESP.	—	—
2.	I believe I have had at least one ESP experience.	—	—
3.	I believe ghosts exist.	—	—
4.	I believe in life after death.	—	—
5.	I believe that some people can contact people who have died.	—	—
6.	I believe that there are flying saucers and people from other places than earth visiting our planet.	—	—
7.	I have had a telepathic experience, where I felt like I was reading another person's thoughts.	—	—
8.	I have had a specific dream about something which matched in detail an event which occurred after my dream. I did not know about the event at the time of the dream and did not expect it.	—	—
9.	I have had the experience of feeling that "I" was outside of or away from my body. This is called an out-of-body experience or astral projection.	—	—
10.	I have seen, heard, or been touched by another being, often referred to as a ghost, and could not explain the experience as being due to a physical or natural cause.	—	—
11.	I have moved an object with my thoughts alone. This is called psychokinesis (PK).	—	—
12.	I have seen light around the body or body parts of another person. As far as I could tell this was not due to a physical or natural cause. This experience is called an aura.	—	—

Demographic Information:

AGE: _____   GENDER: MALE: _____   FEMALE: _____

EXTRASENSORY PERCEPTION (ESP) SURVEY

This is an anonymous survey, conducted as a project for a course in research methods, about your attitudes toward extrasensory perception (ESP) and whether you have had any ESP experiences.

Please check "yes" or "no" to each of the following statements. If you are unsure, check "no". Do not leave any blank.

		Yes	No
1.	I believe in the existence of ESP.	—	—
2.	I believe I have had at least one ESP experience.	—	—
3.	I believe ghosts exist.	—	—
4.	I believe in life after death.	—	—
5.	I believe that some people can contact people who have died.	—	—
6.	I believe that there are flying saucers and people from other places than earth visiting our planet.	—	—
7.	I have had a telepathic experience, where I felt like I was reading another person's thoughts.	—	—
8.	I have had a specific dream about something which matched in detail an event which occurred after my dream. I did not know about the event at the time of the dream and did not expect it.	—	—
9.	I have had the experience of feeling that "I" was outside of or away from my body. This is called an out-of-body experience or astral projection.	—	—
10.	I have seen, heard, or been touched by another being, often referred to as a ghost, and could not explain the experience as being due to a physical or natural cause.	—	—
11.	I have moved an object with my thoughts alone. This is called psychokinesis (PK).	—	—
12.	I have seen light around the body or body parts of another person. As far as I could tell this was not due to a physical or natural cause. This experience is called an aura.	—	—

Demographic Information:

AGE: _____   GENDER: MALE: _____   FEMALE: _____

APPENDIX B

Materials for Topic 7: Ex Post Facto Studies

Laboratory Exercise 2: Gender Differences in Spatial Ability (pp. 75-76)

Mental Rotations Test

This is a test of your ability to look at a drawing of a given object and
find the same object within a set of dissimilar objects. The only difference between the original object and the chosen object will be that
they are presented at different angles. An illustration of this principle
is given below, where the same single object is given in five different
positions. Look at each of them to satisfy yourself that they are only
presented at different angles from one another.

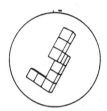 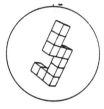 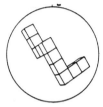 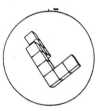 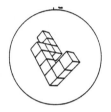

Below are two drawings of new objects. They cannot be made to match the
above five drawings. Please note that you may not turn over the objects.
Satisfy yourself that they are different from the above.

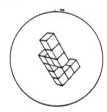 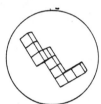

Now let's do some sample problems. For each problem there is a primary
object on the far left. You are to determine which two of four objects to
the right are the same object given on the far left. In each problem
always _two_ of the four drawings are the same object as the one on the left.
You are to put Xs in the boxes below the correct ones, and leave the incorrect ones blank. The first sample problem is done for you.

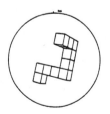 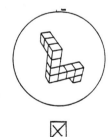 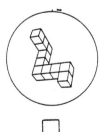  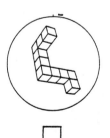

⊠   ☐   ⊠   ☐

Go to the next page

Adapted by S.G. Vandenberg, University of Colorado, July 15, 1971
Revised instructions by H. Crawford, U. of Wyoming, September, 1979

Do the rest of the sample problems yourself. Which two drawings of the four on the right show the same object as the one on the left? There are always two and only two correct answers for each problem. Put an X under the two correct drawings.

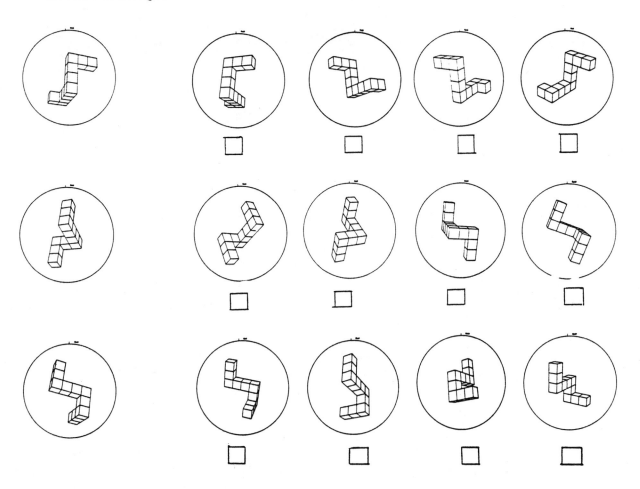

Answers: (1) first and second drawings are correct
(2) first and third drawings are correct
(3) second and third drawings are correct

This test has two parts. You will have <u>3 minutes</u> for each of the two parts. Each part has two pages. When you have finished Part I, STOP. Please do not go one to Part 2 until you are asked to do so. Remember: There are always two and only two correct answers for each item.

Work as quickly as you can without sacraficing accuracy. Your score on this test will reflect both the correct and incorrect responses. Therefore, it will not be to your advantage to guess unless you have some idea which choice is correct.

<u>DO NOT TURN THIS PAGE UNTIL ASKED TO DO SO</u>

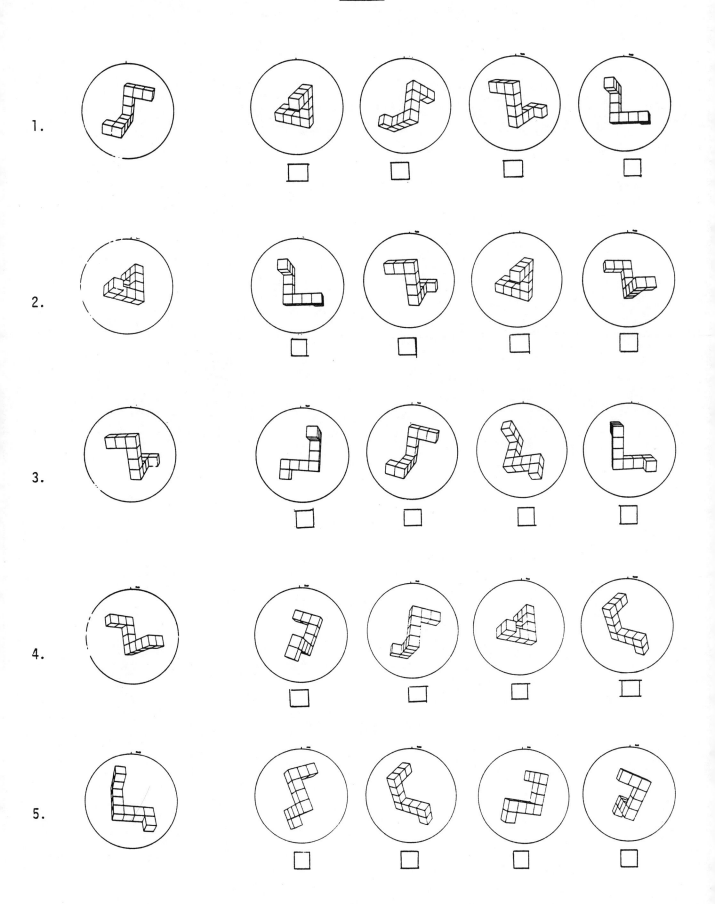

1.

2.

3.

4.

5.

GO ON TO THE NEXT PAGE

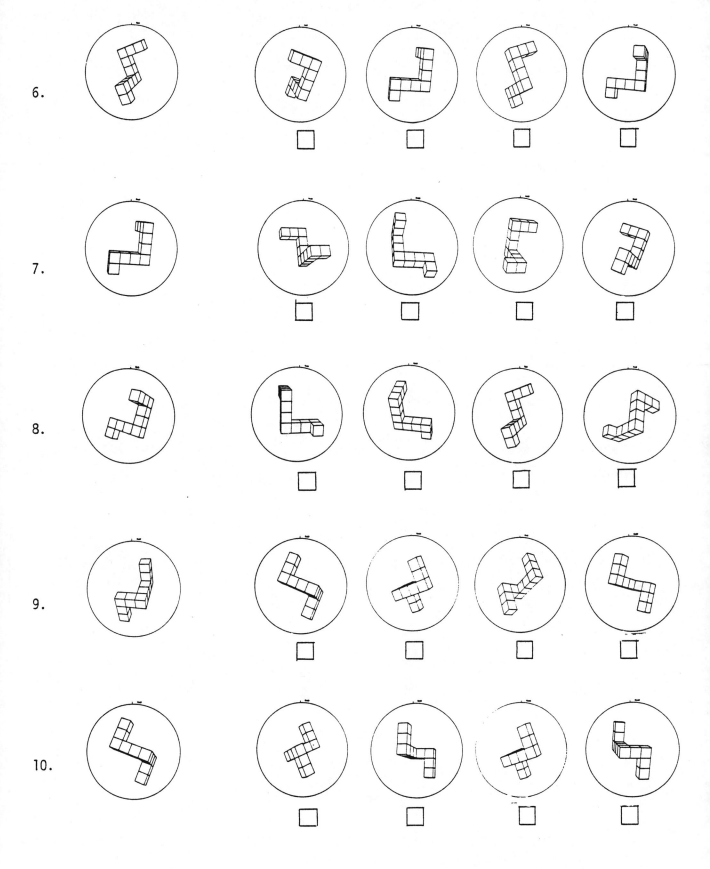

6.

7.

8.

9.

10.

DO NOT TURN THIS PAGE UNTIL ASKED TO DO SO.   STOP

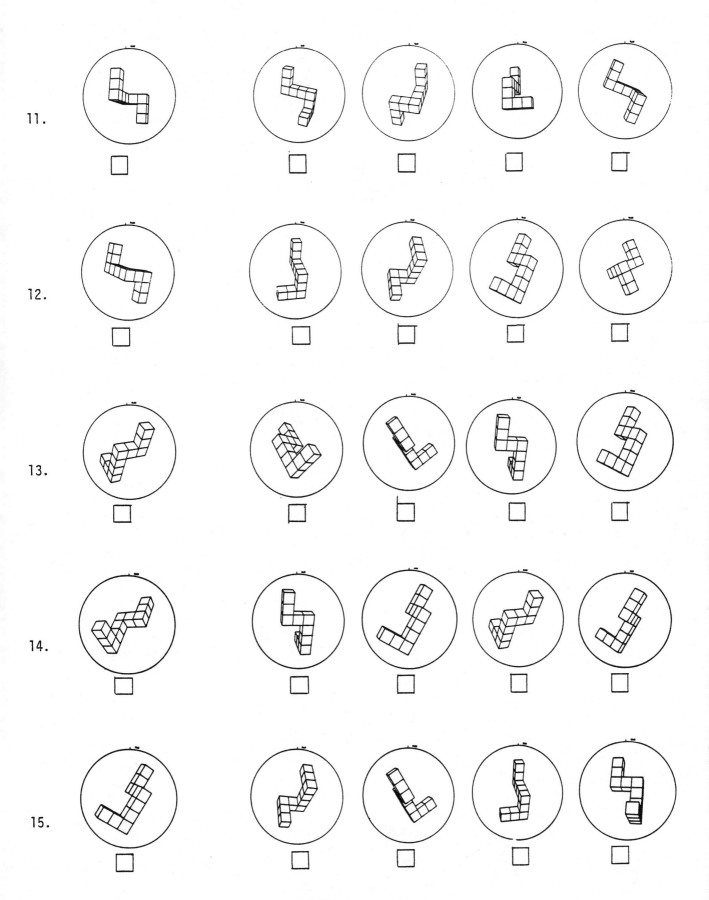

PART II

11.

12.

13.

14.

15.

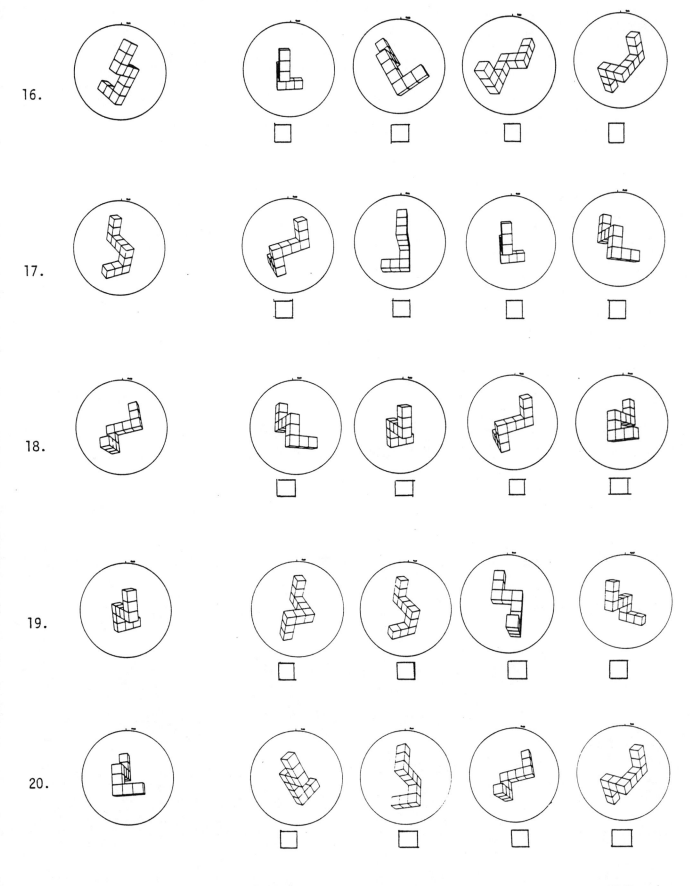

16.

17.

18.

19.

20.

DO NOT TURN THIS PAGE UNTIL ASKED TO DO SO.   STOP

APPENDIX C

Materials for Topic 8: Independent and Dependent Variables

Laboratory Exercise 3: Paired-Associate Learning of Low and High Imagery Words (pp.87-92)

Laboratory Exercise 4: Jury Simulation Research (pp. 93-95)

UNIVERSITY	FISHERMAN	CIRCLE
BODY	DOLLAR	VILLAGE
ELBOW	DIAMOND	CLOCK
MAGAZINE	HAMMER	LETTER
GARDEN	OFFICER	HOUSE

High Response

High Response

High Response

High Response

High Response

High Response

High Response

High Response

High Response

High Response

High Response

High Response

High Response

High Response

High Response

KNOWLEDGE	AGREEMENT	SOUL
CONFIDENCE	FATE	PERMISSION
PATENT	UNIT	EXPRESSION
BELIEF	CHANCE	SENTIMENT
MOMENT	THEORY	QUALITY

Low Response	Low Response	Low Response
Low Response	Low Response	Low Response
Low Response	Low Response	Low Response
Low Response	Low Response	Low Response
Low Response	Low Response	Low Response

This is an anonymous questionnaire to assess the manner in which people judge various offenses. Below is a brief account of a criminal offense. When you have finished reading the case account, you will be asked to give your personal opinion concerning the case. That is, you are to sentence the defendant described in the case account to a specific number of years of imprisonment. Take as much time as you want in reading and contemplating the case before you. Finally, sentence the defendant. Remember that we are interested in your personal opinion, so please give your own personal judgment and not how you feel others might react to the case or how you feel you should react to it. One other thing -- in making your sentence, consider the question of parole as being beyond your jurisdiction. That is, sentence the defendant irrespective of whether or not you feel he should have opportunity for parole after a certain number of years in prison.

John Sander was driving home from an annual Christmas office party on the evening of December 24 when his automobile struck and killed a pedestrian by the name of Martin Lowe. The circumstances leading to this event were as follows: The employees of the insurance office where Sander worked began to party at around 2:00 P.M. on the afternoon of the 24th. By 5:00 P.M. some people were already leaving for home, although many continued to drink and socialize. Sander, who by this time had had several drinks, was offered a lift home by a friend who did not drink and who suggested that Sander leave his car at the office and pick it up when he was in "better shape." Sander declined the offer, claiming he was "stone sober" and would manage fine. By the time Sander had finished another drink, the party was beginning to break up. Sander left the office building and walked to the garage where he had parked his car, a four-door 1965 Chevrolet. It had just started to snow. He wished the garage attendant a Merry Christmas and pulled out into the street. Traffic was very heavy at the time. Sander was six blocks from the garage when he was stopped by a policeman for reckless driving. It was quite apparent to the officer that Sander had been drinking, but rather than give him a ticket on Christmas Eve, he said that he would let Sander off if he would promise to leave his car and take a taxi. Sander agreed. The officer hailed a taxi and Sander got into it. The minute the taxi had turned a corner, however, Sander told the driver to pull over to the curb and let him out. Sander paid the driver and started back to where he had parked his own car. Upon reaching his car he proceeded to start it up and drove off.

He had driven four blocks from the street where the police officer had stopped him when he ran a red light and stuck Lowe, who was crossing the street. Sander immediately stopped the car. Lowe died a few minutes later on the way to the hospital. It was later ascertained that internal hemorrhaging was the cause of death. Sander was apprehended and charged with negligent homicide. The police medical examiner's report indicated that Sander's estimated blood alcohol concentration was between 2.5 and 3.0% at the time of the accident.

Lowe is a noted architect and prominent member of the community. He had designed many well-known buildings throughout the state . . . was an active member of the community welfare board. At the time of the incident, Lowe was on his way to the Lincoln Orphanage, of which he was a founding member, with Christmas gifts. He is survived by his wife and two children, ages 11 and 15. Sander is a sixty-four-year-old insurance adjustor who has been employed by the same insurance firm for 42 years. Sander was friendly with everyone and was known as a good worker. Sander is a widower, his wife having died of cancer the previous year, and he is, consequently, spending Christmas Eve with his son and daughter-in-law. When the incident occurred, Sander's leg banged the steering column, reaggravating a gun wound which had been the source of a slight limp and much pain. Sander's traffic record shows he has received three tickets in the past five years, two of which were moving violations.

Sander was charged with negligent automobile homicide, a crime which in the state is punishable by imprisonment of one to twenty-five years.

Your job is to determine how many years of imprisonment, according to your own judgement, he should receive. After you have considered the case presented on the previous page, note below how many years of imprisonment you, as judge, would give him. Parole is beyond your jurisdiction. That is, sentence the defendant irrespective of whether or not you feel he should have opportunity for parole after a certain number of years in prison.

NUMBER OF YEARS _____

Now, would you indicate your impression of the defendant and the victim on the following scale. Circle the number which is closest to your impression of each person.

SANDERS;

| extremely | | | | | | | | | extremely |

| 1 2 3 4 5 6 7 8 9

favorable   unfavorable

LOWE:

extremely   extremely

1 2 3 4 5 6 7 8 9

favorable   unfavorable

What issues did you think were important in deciding the length of imprisonment?

What is your age? _____   Gender: Male _____   Female _____

Thank you very much for your participation. Please put this in the envelope the interviewer has so that your questionnaire will remain completely anonymous.

(1)

This is an anonymous questionnaire to assess the manner in which people judge various offenses. Below is a brief account of a criminal offense. When you have finished reading the case account, you will be asked to give your personal opinion concerning the case. That is, you are to sentence the defendant described in the case account to a specific number of years of imprisonment. Take as much time as you want in reading and contemplating the case before you. Finally, sentence the defendant. Remember that we are interested in your personal opinion, so please give your own personal judgment and not how you feel others might react to the case or how you feel you should react to it. One other thing -- in making your sentence, consider the question of parole as being beyond your jurisdiction. That is, sentence the defendant irrespective of whether or not you feel he should have opportunity for parole after a certain number of years in prison.

John Sander was driving home from an annual Christmas office party on the evening of December 24 when his automobile struck and killed a pedestrian by the name of Martin Lowe. The circumstances leading to this event were as follows: The employees of the insurance office where Sander worked began to party at around 2:00 P.M. on the afternoon of the 24th. By 5:00 P.M. some people were already leaving for home, although many continued to drink and socialize. Sander, who by this time had had several drinks, was offered a lift home by a friend who did not drink and who suggested that Sander leave his car at the office and pick it up when he was in "better shape." Sander declined the offer, claiming he was "stone sober" and would manage fine. By the time Sander had finished another drink, the party was beginning to break up. Sander left the office building and walked to the garage where he had parked his car, a four-door 1965 Chevrolet. It had just started to snow. He wished the garage attendant a Merry Christmas and pulled out into the street. Traffic was very heavy at the time. Sander was six blocks from the garage when he was stopped by a policeman for reckless driving. It was quite apparent to the officer that Sander had been drinking, but rather than give him a ticket on Christmas Eve, he said that he would let Sander off if he would promise to leave his car and take a taxi. Sander agreed. The officer hailed a taxi and Sander got into it. The minute the taxi had turned a corner, however, Sander told the driver to pull over to the curb and let him out. Sander paid the driver and started back to where he had parked his own car. Upon reaching his car he proceeded to start it up and drove off.

He had driven four blocks from the street where the police officer had stopped him when he ran a red light and stuck Lowe, who was crossing the street. Sander immediately stopped the car. Lowe died a few minutes later on the way to the hospital. It was later ascertained that internal hemorrhaging was the cause of death. Sander was apprehended and charged with negligent homicide. The police medical examiner's report indicated that Sander's estimated blood alcohol concentration was between 2.5 and 3.0% at the time of the accident.

Lowe is a notorious gangster and syndicate boss who had been vying for power in the syndicate controlling the state's underworld activities. He was best known for his alleged responsibility in the Riverview massacre of five men. At the time of the incident, Lowe was carrying a loaded 32-caliber pistol which was found on his body. He had been out of jail on bond, awaiting trial on a double indictment of mail fraud and income tax evasion. Sander is a sixty-four-year-old insurance adjustor who has been employed by the same insurance firm for 42 years. Sander was friendly with everyone and was known as a good worker. Sander is a widower, his wife having died of cancer the previous year, and he is, consequently, spending Christmas Eve with his son and daughter-in-law. When the incident occurred, Sander's leg banged the steering column, reaggravating a gun wound which had been the source of a slight limp and much pain. Sander's traffic record shows he has received three tickets in the past five years, two of which were moving violations.

Sander was charged with negligent automobile homicide, a crime which in the state is punishable by imprisonment of one to twenty-five years.

Your job is to determine how many years of imprisonment, according to your own judgement, he should receive. After you have considered the case presented on the previous page, note below how many years of imprisonment you, as judge, would give him. Parole is beyond your jurisdiction. That is, sentence the defendant irrespective of whether or not you feel he should have opportunity for parole after a certain number of years in prison.

NUMBER OF YEARS _____

Now, would you indicate your impression of the defendant and the victim on the following scale. Circle the number which is closest to your impression of each person.

SANDERS;

extremely									extremely
	1	2	3	4	5	6	7	8	9
favorable									unfavorable

LOWE:

extremely									extremely
	1	2	3	4	5	6	7	8	9
favorable									unfavorable

What issues did you think were important in deciding the length of imprisonment?

What is your age? _____   Gender: Male _____   Female _____

Thank you very much for your participation. Please put this in the envelope the interviewer has so that your questionnaire will remain completely anonymous.

This is an anonymous questionnaire to assess the manner in which people judge various offenses. Below is a brief account of a criminal offense. When you have finished reading the case account, you will be asked to give your personal opinion concerning the case. That is, you are to sentence the defendant described in the case account to a specific number of years of imprisonment. Take as much time as you want in reading and contemplating the case before you. Finally, sentence the defendant. Remember that we are interested in your personal opinion, so please give your own personal judgment and not how you feel others might react to the case or how you feel you should react to it. One other thing -- in making your sentence, consider the question of parole as being beyond your jurisdiction. That is, sentence the defendant irrespective of whether or not you feel he should have opportunity for parole after a certain number of years in prison.

John Sander was driving home from an annual Christmas office party on the evening of December 24 when his automobile struck and killed a pedestrian by the name of Martin Lowe. The circumstances leading to this event were as follows: The employees of the insurance office where Sander worked began to party at around 2:00 P.M. on the afternoon of the 24th. By 5:00 P.M. some people were already leaving for home, although many continued to drink and socialize. Sander, who by this time had had several drinks, was offered a lift home by a friend who did not drink and who suggested that Sander leave his car at the office and pick it up when he was in "better shape." Sander declined the offer, claiming he was "stone sober" and would manage fine. By the time Sander had finished another drink, the party was beginning to break up. Sander left the office building and walked to the garage where he had parked his car, a four-door 1965 Chevrolet. It had just started to snow. He wished the garage attendant a Merry Christmas and pulled out into the street. Traffic was very heavy at the time. Sander was six blocks from the garage when he was stopped by a policeman for reckless driving. It was quite apparent to the officer that Sander had been drinking, but rather than give him a ticket on Christmas Eve, he said that he would let Sander off if he would promise to leave his car and take a taxi. Sander agreed. The officer hailed a taxi and Sander got into it. The minute the taxi had turned a corner, however, Sander told the driver to pull over to the curb and let him out. Sander paid the driver and started back to where he had parked his own car. Upon reaching his car he proceeded to start it up and drove off.

He had driven four blocks from the street where the police officer had stopped him when he ran a red light and stuck Lowe, who was crossing the street. Sander immediately stopped the car. Lowe died a few minutes later on the way to the hospital. It was later ascertained that internal hemorrhaging was the cause of death. Sander was apprehended and charged with negligent homicide. The police medical examiner's report indicated that Sander's estimated blood alcohol concentration was between 2.5 and 3.0% at the time of the accident.

Lowe is a noted architect and prominent member of the community. He had designed many well-known buildings throughout the state . . . was an active member of the community welfare board. At the time of the incident, Lowe was on his way to the Lincoln Orphanage, of which he was a founding member, with Christmas gifts. He is survived by his wife and two children, ages 11 and 15. Sander is a thirty-three-year-old janitor. In the building where Sander has been working as a janitor for the past two months, he was not known by many of the firm employees, but was nevertheless invited to join the party. Sander is a two-time divorcee, with three children by his first wife, who has since remarried. He was going to spend Christmas Eve with his girlfriend in her apartment. The effect of the incident on Sander was negligible; he was slightly shaken up by the impact, but suffered no major injuries. Sander has two misdemeanors on his criminal record in the past five years -- breaking and entering and a drug violation. His traffic record shows three tickets in the same space of time.

Sander was charged with negligent automobile homicide, a crime which in the state is punishable by imprisonment of one to twenty-five years.

Your job is to determine how many years of imprisonment, according to your own judgement, he should receive. After you have considered the case presented on the previous page, note below how many years of imprisonment you, as judge, would give him. Parole is beyond your jurisdiction. That is, sentence the defendant irrespective of whether or not you feel he should have opportunity for parole after a certain number of years in prison.

NUMBER OF YEARS _____

Now, would you indicate your impression of the defendant and the victim on the following scale. Circle the number which is closest to your impression of each person.

SANDERS;

| extremely | | | | | | | | | extremely |
| favorable | 1 | 2 | 3 | 4 | 5 | 6 | 7 | 8 | 9 unfavorable |

LOWE:

| extremely | | | | | | | | | extremely |
| favorable | 1 | 2 | 3 | 4 | 5 | 6 | 7 | 8 | 9 unfavorable |

What issues did you think were important in deciding the length of imprisonment?

What is your age? _____   Gender: Male _____   Female _____

Thank you very much for your participation. Please put this in the envelope the interviewer has so that your questionnaire will remain completely anonymous.

(3)

This is an anonymous questionnaire to assess the manner in which people judge various offenses. Below is a brief account of a criminal offense. When you have finished reading the case account, you will be asked to give your personal opinion concerning the case. That is, you are to sentence the defendant described in the case account to a specific number of years of imprisonment. Take as much time as you want in reading and contemplating the case before you. Finally, sentence the defendant. Remember that we are interested in your personal opinion, so please give your own personal judgment and not how you feel others might react to the case or how you feel you should react to it. One other thing -- in making your sentence, consider the question of parole as being beyond your jurisdiction. That is, sentence the defendant irrespective of whether or not you feel he should have opportunity for parole after a certain number of years in prison.

John Sander was driving home from an annual Christmas office party on the evening of December 24 when his automobile struck and killed a pedestrian by the name of Martin Lowe. The circumstances leading to this event were as follows: The employees of the insurance office where Sander worked began to party at around 2:00 P.M. on the afternoon of the 24th. By 5:00 P.M. some people were already leaving for home, although many continued to drink and socialize. Sander, who by this time had had several drinks, was offered a lift home by a friend who did not drink and who suggested that Sander leave his car at the office and pick it up when he was in "better shape." Sander declined the offer, claiming he was "stone sober" and would manage fine. By the time Sander had finished another drink, the party was beginning to break up. Sander left the office building and walked to the garage where he had parked his car, a four-door 1965 Chevrolet. It had just started to snow. He wished the garage attendant a Merry Christmas and pulled out into the street. Traffic was very heavy at the time. Sander was six blocks from the garage when he was stopped by a policeman for reckless driving. It was quite apparent to the officer that Sander had been drinking, but rather than give him a ticket on Christmas Eve, he said that he would let Sander off if he would promise to leave his car and take a taxi. Sander agreed. The officer hailed a taxi and Sander got into it. The minute the taxi had turned a corner, however, Sander told the driver to pull over to the curb and let him out. Sander paid the driver and started back to where he had parked his own car. Upon reaching his car he proceeded to start it up and drove off.

He had driven four blocks from the street where the police officer had stopped him when he ran a red light and stuck Lowe, who was crossing the street. Sander immediately stopped the car. Lowe died a few minutes later on the way to the hospital. It was later ascertained that internal hemorrhaging was the cause of death. Sander was apprehended and charged with negligent homicide. The police medical examiner's report indicated that Sander's estimated blood alcohol concentration was between 2.5 and 3.0% at the time of the accident.

Lowe is a notorious gangster and syndicate boss who had been vying for power in the syndicate controlling the state's underworld activities. He was best known for his alleged responsibility in the Riverview massacre of five men. At the time of the incident, Lowe was carrying a loaded 32-caliber pistol which was found on his body. He had been out of jail on bond, awaiting trial on a double indictment of mail fraud and income tax evasion. Sander is a thirty-three-year-old janitor. In the building where Sander has been working as a janitor for the past two months, he was not known by many of the firm employees, but was nevertheless invited to join the party. Sander is a two-time divorcee, with three children by his first wife, who has since remarried. He was going to spend Christmas Eve with his girlfriend in her apartment. The effect of the incident on Sander was negligible; he was slightly shaken up by the impact, but suffered no major injuries. Sander has two misdemeanors on his criminal record in the past five years -- breaking and entering and a drug violation. His traffic record shows three tickets in the same space of time.

Sander was charged with negligent automobile homicide, a crime which in the state is punishable by imprisonment of one to twenty-five years.

Your job is to determine how many years of imprisonment, according to your own judgement, he should receive. After you have considered the case presented on the previous page, note below how many years of imprisonment you, as judge, would give him. Parole is beyond your jurisdiction. That is, sentence the defendant irrespective of whether or not you feel he should have opportunity for parole after a certain number of years in prison.

NUMBER OF YEARS _____

Now, would you indicate your impression of the defendant and the victim on the following scale. Circle the number which is closest to your impression of each person.

SANDERS;

extremely   extremely
favorable   1   2   3   4   5   6   7   8   9 unfavorable

LOWE:

extremely   extremely
favorable   1   2   3   4   5   6   7   8   9 unfavorable

What issues did you think were important in deciding the length of imprisonment?

What is your age? _____   Gender: Male _____   Female _____

Thank you very much for your participation. Please put this in the envelope the interviewer has so that your questionnaire will remain completely anonymous.

NOTES

NOTES

NOTES

NOTES